Wendy Griffis joined our business coaching program at Buffini & Company in 2007. She has always impressed me as someone who embodies what it means to be a true professional in this industry. She's a life-long learner who takes the time to care for customers while understanding what it takes to build a business for the long-term. Wendy has integrity, operates with excellence, and has the utmost professionalism.

—Brian Buffini

Founder and chairman, Buffini & Company

Extraordinary relational qualities are seldom seen in action, both professionally and personally in tandem, and consistently over time! Author, mentor, trainer and top producing realtor, Wendy Griffis makes the "good life" seem attainable for all. Her attention to detail, outstanding customer care, and ability to connect and collaborate bring success to her clients, partners, and friends!

—Carole Souza

Realtor

Life and business coach, BCC, Friends & Family Home Group

Better Homes & Gardens RE

The Good Life Group

Wendy is a rock star realtor who is always looking for new ways to bring value to her clients. She has built her business on relationships and trust. I've had the pleasure of working with Wendy over the past year and I have learned a great deal of what makes an incredible realtor. Now you have an opportunity to discover these vital traits as well. Wendy's book is a must-read for anyone who is currently buying a home or who is planning to buy a home in the future. Wendy breaks down the seven traits of a great realtor in an easy and understandable format. I enjoyed reading the real-life stories which provide context for the traits. I now feel confident that I have the tools to find the perfect realtor.

—Manny Torres

Brand strategist, Rock My Image

Co-author, *Amplify Your Business: The Rockstar Professional's Guide to Marketing Success*

Your purpose in life is to be referable. No matter who you are or what you do, you should seek to be referred, to be the most recommended person. As an entrepreneur, business owner, or Realtor, you should seek to build a referable business. Otherwise, what are you doing wrong? It takes character, competence, and communication to be the most referred person or most recommended business. Wendy addresses all these completely and concisely in her chapters on the seven key traits in *Recognize the Difference*. Bottom Line: *Recognize the Difference* is the book consumers should read before working with an agent. *Recognize the Difference* is the book agents should read before working with consumers.

—Michael J. Maher

Author, *(7L) The Seven Levels of Communication*; *The Miracle Morning for Real Estate Agents*
CEO, REFERCO
Publisher, *REFERRALS Magazine*
Host, *REFERRALS Podcast*

Recognize the Difference is a great read with really good insights to consider that hadn't even crossed my mind before. Throughout the book there are helpful insights that can make a huge difference when choosing who to work with when making one of the most important decisions in your life. Another thing I really like about the book is how it makes helpful information interesting. Wendy Griffis is an amazing realtor who goes all-in to help her clients, and you really get a sense of who she is by reading this book. Even if you've worked with a real estate professional before, I recommend giving this book a read; you'll learn something new for certain that can benefit your future decisions.

—Kenny Harper

Marketing advisor
CEO, Rock My Image
Author, *Amplified Business Breakthroughs*; *Own Your Habits, Rock Your Life.*

It's rare that you come across such a loyal, practical person like Wendy Griffis. She has a veracious appetite for learning and is genuinely interested in impacting others with that learning. Wendy's ridiculous drive for excellence shines apparent to all those who get to experience her vast wisdom and outside the box mindset. *Recognize the Difference* is her calling card to help others join in her vision.

—Darrin Jackson

Certified business coach, Buffini & Company

Wendy Griffis understands the difference in the level of professionalism needed for success in the real estate industry. In *Recognize the Difference*, she clearly provides to the consumer what they should be looking for in their real estate agent. In particular, she gets that real estate sales is all about lifestyle and consumer experience. Her transparency and business-savvy come through clearly and is a must-read for anyone considering hiring a real estate agent.

—Sherry Chris

CEO, president, and head visionary, Better Homes and Garden Real Estate

RECOGNIZE THE DIFFERENCE

RECOGNIZE
THE
DIFFERENCE

· · · · ● · · ·

7 KEY TRAITS

to ensure the best real estate

agent experience

Wendy Griffis

Advantage.

Published by Advantage, Charleston, South Carolina.
Member of Advantage Media Group.

ADVANTAGE is a registered trademark, and the Advantage colophon is a trademark of Advantage Media Group, Inc.

Printed in the United States of America.

10 9 8 7 6 5 4 3 2 1

ISBN: 978-1-64225-063-3
LCCN: 2019931048

Cover design by Melanie Cloth.
Layout design by Megan Elger.

This publication is designed to provide accurate and authoritative information in regard to the subject matter covered. It is sold with the understanding that the publisher is not engaged in rendering legal, accounting, or other professional services. If legal advice or other expert assistance is required, the services of a competent professional person should be sought.

Advantage Media Group is proud to be a part of the Tree Neutral® program. Tree Neutral offsets the number of trees consumed in the production and printing of this book by taking proactive steps such as planting trees in direct proportion to the number of trees used to print books. To learn more about Tree Neutral, please visit **www.treeneutral.com**.

Advantage Media Group is a publisher of business, self-improvement, and professional development books and online learning. We help entrepreneurs, business leaders, and professionals share their Stories, Passion, and Knowledge to help others Learn & Grow. Do you have a manuscript or book idea that you would like us to consider for publishing? Please visit **advantagefamily.com** or call **1.866.775.1696**.

*I would like to dedicate this book to Jason,
my wonderful loving husband, who has been my
biggest supporter, my co-dreamer, and always
encourages me to go after my goals.*

TABLE OF CONTENTS

FOREWORD BY JOSH FORSTER

I am large proponent of knowing your purpose in everything that you do—your "why" so to speak. Having known Wendy for many years now it has been wonderful to see her develop her *why* to the point where she felt the need to write it down in the pages of this book.

You see, Wendy weathered the storm of the greatest recession since the great depression in one of the worst-hit states in our country. Florida was essentially one of our ground zeros for plummeting real estate values. Real estate agents were one of the professions that got hit hard as well. Not only were they losing their homes right along with the rest of their neighbors, but their jobs and businesses were tied to an industry that was dying on the vine.

As a result, agents were getting out of the business by the thousands and hundreds of thousands. The real estate industry has seen this cycle before. When markets are fast and it seems like homes are selling themselves, people jump into the business looking for an easy paycheck. Not only do the checks not come, but as soon as the market turns, they jump right back out again. Good people, but people that did not have the skills to withstand such a downturn the recession provided.

But not Wendy. Wendy survived and is thriving in the real estate industry in Jacksonville. Wendy credits many things with being able to stick through the recession, but some of the largest things that got her through were her relationships with other professional real estate agents. Together, they developed and honed their skills and got through it. As a result, they are now some of the most skilled and seasoned agents that know how to work and succeed in all types of markets.

This has become Wendy's "why." Her passion. To help teach those skills to other agents. And now, through this book, to show those skills to homeowners (or those who hope to be), and to help elevate a profession that has traditionally not had a good reputation.

There is a massive difference in the professionalism and skill set of real estate agents out there. What Wendy has done with this book is inform you on not only what those differences are, but how to recognize those differences. To be able to differentiate the good from the bad, and reap the benefits because of it.

Josh Forster

Author of *Discovering Why,* national speaker, owner of Elevations Real Estate.

ACKNOWLEDGMENTS

The journey to writing this book came from unexpected sources. As a young, newer agent, listening to Brian Buffini and his vision for the professionalism in the real estate industry, and following his success principals through trainings, events, and podcasts, was very impactful. My coach, Darrin Jackson, and my collaboration with peers—Josh Forster, A.B. Priceman, Jordan Hayward, Gail Long, Dennis Kinkopf, Jane Evans, Philip Thompson, Trey Clark, Jeanne Pilcher, Kavie and Christian Stahl, Yvette Barton, Chris Levchuk, Maureen Dunn, Erin Marler, Katie Tarpley, Judy Moran, and Michael Morris—became the foundation for which I grew my strength of character, real estate skills, and leadership muscles.

Years later, as a trainer and leader in the real estate space, I could see clearly the different approaches to running a real estate business, and how we connect to the consumer. Old school sales techniques and cold calling were outdated models and were typically disliked by the consumers on the receiving end. I knew there had to be a better way. Geoff Burt and Dan McCarthy took a chance on my real estate office/company vision of building a real estate company model where the agents took a relational approach to working with their clients, and we began the journey with an even deeper collaboration and synergy with Teri Davis, Joey Gabriel, Dawn Sutherland, Karen Crede, Amy McBride, Tracie Porreca, Shanon Bond, Denise Davis, Betsy McNeil, Cammie Thomas, Pushpa Devi, John Magnusson, and Daniel Lewis. This team of amazing agents gave me their trust, and it deepened my commitment to the industry. Not to mention, over the last several years, I've been able to connect and share with so many outstanding agents, both within my local market and outside of it—this group of professional agents is too lengthy to list, but you know who you are!

By a chance referral, I met the authors of the book *Amplify Your Business*, Manny Torres, Jen Richter, and Kenny Harper, who inspired me to "claim my stage." Until then, I felt I had a lot to share, but lacked the confidence to step into the spot light. Once I did, I found that what I had to say helped others, had value, and my peers encouraged me to take action. Michael Maher taught me the courage to not play small. And he said that if I ever wrote a book including ideas of a generosity generation, he would be on board. That planted a seed. Could I actually write a book? Ultimately, I have to thank the publisher and editors at Advantage Media Group|ForbesBooks for listening to my ideas, helping me devise an outline, and making what I felt drawn to share a legitimate offering to the consumer. Without their guidance and direction, this would still be notes on a legal pad.

Thanks to the many clients who participated in my survey and interviews, without which I wouldn't have the perspective of what it is like to be on the other side of me and my real estate group. I'm forever in your gratitude.

Lastly, I have to thank my marketing team and staff who help me every day to elevate our services to our clients and support our group so we can strive to be the best and live by these principals. Particularly Marybeth Baumann and Julie Haines—without you, the vision could not be possible, the lessons learned, and the time carved out would be missing, and this book would never have happened!

ABOUT THE AUTHOR

Wendy Griffis is a top producing REALTOR® and group leader, entrepreneur, speaker, and author. As of 2018, Wendy was ranked number fourteen of the Top Twenty-Five Real Estate Agents in the Jacksonville Journal Book of Lists. Her experience and understanding of the real estate market allows her to give accurate and thorough advice to clients, providing successful, streamlined results in any type of market conditions. She has built her business by referral, and gaining this recommendation is contingent on providing unparalleled council and service. Having a healthy referral business means that she goes the extra mile to ensure that each client feels secure endorsing her services to other friends and family.

Wendy was featured on the cover of *Jacksonville Real Producers* magazine and honored for her passion for elevating the real estate profession. Wendy was also featured in articles in *Florida Realtor* and *Buffini & Company* magazines. Wendy is a founding member of Michael J. Maher's Certified Referral Trainer Academy, has been a *Buffini & Company* member since 2006, and a training ambassador for their company since 2011. Because of her "Relationships are more important than transactions," and "Repeat and referral," business plan, Wendy has skyrocketed her business throughout the years. She brings her experience as an advisor, negotiator, mentor, and trainer to benefit her clients and fellow agents. Wendy shares her path to success and the practical "how to" to help agents have a business that not only feeds their family, but also feeds their soul—a method to achieve not only success, but also significance. Sharing her client-centric model with agents, and now to the consumer through this book, she lets out the secret to explain the solid foundation of her business.

Wendy is a graduate of University of North Florida with a degree in statistics and business administration. Wendy's family includes her husband, Jason, son Kyle, and two fur babies named Parko and Mishka.

NOTE FROM THE AUTHOR

Recently, I surveyed some of my past clients with this question: "Before working with the Wendy Griffis Group, what was your perception of real estate agents?"

A part of me, I think, knew what to expect, yet, reading their responses shocked me!

Here are some of the things they wrote:

"Pushy like a used car salesperson."

"Not worth the cost."

"Of little use or help."

"Making a lot of money for very little work."

"Salesy."

"Only interested in making a quick sale."

"Scrappy."

"Bossy and over paid."

"Self-focused, not customer focused."

"Glamourous, fun, easy job."

All this about the industry I've worked in since 2000, through all the ups, downs, and challenges of being an entrepreneur. An industry I love, have journeyed with friends and co-workers through—people who also feel just as passionately about serving clients at the highest level.

I've worked with many clients over the years in hopes of changing this perception. But not enough! After reviewing these remarks, I knew that I had to figure out a way to communicate that not all agents fit within these stereotypes.

In fact, many of my coworkers aren't anything like the people described in the survey responses. Yet studies continually show that real estate agents rank low on the list of trusted professionals.

It's true that poor performers and unethical people are present in all professions. Regrettably, it is those select few who muddy the reputation of all who practice in the profession—real estate being no exception. But I'd beg to ask, are all car salesman bad, unethical people perched to rip you off? The answer is, in fact, no, although the profession has a bad rap because of the few who do exactly that. The same is true of real estate.

The fact is, there are many more who don't fit into these stereotypes than those who actually do. But, as they say, it only takes a few bad apples to spoil the barrel.

But to be fair, looking at it from the customer's standpoint, how can you tell apart skilled agents who actually care about their clients from the cheesy low-skilled salespeople who are only interested in their bottom lines?

That's when the idea started to formulate in my mind. It started with a simple question: How can I help the general public recognize a true professional without them having to rely on false or misleading marketing tactics from disingenuous agents? And along came the premise of this book: How to identify a true, sincere, compassionate, trustworthy professional service person in the real estate industry.

I interviewed several clients to capture their stories and experiences to give you a sense of what the skills of good, honest agents could look like in action.

My goal for this book is to educate the consumer and give them the knowledge they need to feel confident they aren't working with a "sleazy salesperson." I'll spill the secrets on what to look for in an agent and the seven distinguishing factors that will indicate you're working with a true pro. These characteristics, I hope you'll realize, will make hiring a good real estate agent worth every penny—and more. Because when you identify them, you'll find that these agents are genuinely in it for you, not just their commission.

READ THIS BOOK BEFORE YOU USE AN ONLINE/ DISCOUNT AGENT OR TECH SOLUTION

Have you noticed an increase in real estate "ads" on TV and social media feeds? Pretty much everywhere you turn, there's a technology company trying to persuade you that they are the new solution to buying or selling a home. Tech disrupters are making bold claims, attacking traditional models of agent support, and predicting their demise. This, of course, is nothing new, particularly during booming real estate markets. But this boom, coupled with improvements in technology, has caught the eye of the venture capitalists. Since the value of homes in the US has reached record levels, it seems only fair to assume that big players with deep pockets want a piece of that pie. And I may be a little biased in that comment, because to be honest, though I am not a venture capitalist, I do benefit from the real estate market, too. The catch is, many of these well-financed companies fail to realize that there's more to a real estate transaction than scheduling a showing, and clicking a button and filling out an offer form, even with "help" from an online real estate agent source. If you get any guidance at all from these "agents," you still run the risk of getting someone who may not offer you the value and quality of service the industry demands.

Disruptors or Distractors

Although these venture capitalists working to change how real estate is bought and sold like to consider themselves "disruptors," I think of them more as distractors, because they're missing one crucial skill—most of them have never helped anyone buy or sell a home. The other part of the problem is that simplifying the process into an online one isn't so easy, and I'll explain why later.

These distractors show up in the form of "discount" or "cash back" real estate companies. I've seen these companies come and go, usually appearing during a boom and disappearing shortly thereafter. The reason they trend in and out this way is this: Typically, since they're offering a discount, these companies have to make up the costs and profits in volume. They often hire struggling real estate agents who aren't particularly experienced or skilled. When these agents are willing to give away their income to grab a piece of the client real estate pie, you have to question how skilled they really are, or how much they're in it for the customers versus for building a volume transaction-based business to make up for the lower fees. Occasionally, these companies are good for agents who are only focused on the financial aspect of a real estate transaction. But often a consumer, in an effort to try and "save" money, ends up spending more or losing more than if they'd hired a profes-sional in the first place. Or even worse, they incur high risks during the process because they don't have skilled representation.

The reality is, if you were involved in a legal battle, or if you needed a doctor, you would want to choose the best professional, even if they cost more. But because real estate agents are often seen as being "one and the same," it's no surprise that consumers are swayed by more wallet-friendly opportunities. And that's what I hope to clearly educate you on: some real estate agents are different. There are ways to tell the good ones from the mediocre ones, and once you have that knowledge, you can make an educated decision in choosing one based on what matters to you.

Don't get me wrong, online real estate resources like these aren't entirely bad. To be clear, I'm not for eliminating them. I love how technology can be used to enhance the real estate process (which I'll elaborate on later), but it should be used to support the process, not replace it. What I am for is educating the consumer that whom they choose to work with matters.

Let's Talk Real Estate.

The question of whom to choose when buying or selling a home is on a lot of people's minds—as I'm sure you know since you picked up this book in the first place. Of course, being an agent, whether I'm out and about meeting new people or hanging out with old friends, the conversation often turns to real estate. But I find that real estate is also something that people talk about all the time, regardless of whether or not there's an agent present in the conversation or not, because everyone is interested in what's going on with their home and investments.

There are three traditional basic human needs: food, clothing, and shelter. I just happen to be in the shelter business. So, whether someone is completely happy with where they're living or if they're looking to make a move, we all have a vested interest in what's going on with our shelters (homes). Additionally, for those who invest in real estate or own more than one property, these investments are often their biggest assets, so they care about what's happening with them.

Therefore, unless you're in the minority and don't care about the real estate market, you've probably at least heard some buzz surrounding the industry and what's trending with buyers and sellers in the marketplace. And if you're like many people I know (myself included), you've probably given thought to saving money and may believe there are cheaper ways to buy and sell real estate. In all transparency, yes, there are cheaper ways. But in this particular industry, cheaper does not often equate to more money in your pocket, a better deal, or an easier process.

The truth is, understanding the real estate process is a much more-involved decision than asking, "How much is it going to cost?" Instead, the question should be, "Who am I going to use and why?" It's easy to go online, see a home you like, and click on the first person who has a bunch of stars on their review. Or mistakenly reach out to the listing agent and unknowingly get locked in, only to later struggle with how to "break up" with them.

The reason this often happens to people is that many of these online resources mislead consumers, driving them to see things they want them to see based on the company's "algorithms." For instance, the site may enable pop-ups featuring one or more agents while the consumer is viewing a property. Those agents often pay to be advertised this way and aren't necessarily the best fit for the consumer. Choosing an agent through a tech or discount site is as good as rolling dice; you may go in thinking you're making a simple inquiry, but really your information is being fed into an agent's "lead system," and you just don't know the skills (or lack thereof) of the agent on the other side.

The 80/20 Rule

The good news is there are many great real estate agents out there. But, as with most things in life, there's always the 80/20 rule, which states that 20 percent of the people derive 80 percent of the results. In the real estate space, that number can get convoluted because many online agents pay to show up first in search results. So, are they good at what they do, or are they simply good at marketing themselves? Will they hand you off to an entry-level team member? Are they just pouring money into "positioning" themselves on properties that aren't theirs? Believe it or not, many large real estate marketing sites are managed this way. Time and time again, I hear people say, "I thought I was talking to the listing agent," when in reality, nothing is further from the truth.

I believe consumers deserve transparency online, but with ads and agents paying for position marketing, the whole picture grows distorted for consumers.

Of course, there are times when these sites can be useful in helping educate people about property details. If you're looking for an overall high-level overview, these sites can also help you glean information about homes and the current market situation.

What concerns me, however, is the dirty little secret behind them: they're used by agents and big companies to generate leads. There's nothing wrong with agents promoting themselves to generate business—as long as the consumer is fully educated about just whom they're asking for help. Most of the time, people want to learn more about the homes they're viewing, but little do they realize that the agent answering the inquiry on the other end has never even seen the home themselves. They've just paid to position themselves as the first person the potential client sees/hears from, so they can "capture" the client.

You might already be able to see why there's value in finding an agent who can counsel you on your unique situation to maximize your position. And, though many of the technology disruptor talking points often make people feel that all agents are the same and a discount or online agent is equal to someone who provides full service, I'm here to say that there's a big difference.

Why Take My Word for It?

I've been an agent since 2000, and although all agents are new to the business at the start of their careers and deserve a chance to shine, it's more imperative now more than ever to make sure you're working with someone highly trained. I've experienced the ups and downs of the industry, and I know what it takes to build a successful practice that connects with consumers in a meaningful way that understands them and their unique needs. An agent should offer personalized advice and exceptional service in order to provide peace of mind, clarity, and tangible results to clients.

> **An agent should offer personalized advice and exceptional service in order to provide peace of mind, clarity, and tangible results to clients.**

There are seven traits of a highly trained and experienced professional agent—which we'll discuss in detail later—and once you understand those, you'll be able to discern how to choose a real estate agent who offers accurate and insightful advice. You'll learn how to select someone who will use an honest and direct approach (by not always telling you what you want to hear, but rather what you need to hear) and focus less on selling you something and more on serving your goals. This level of knowledge is exactly what you'll get from this book. Armed with this information, it is my hope that you'll have a better understanding of what you should look for and what separates the mediocre agents from the incredible ones. With my insight and knowledge as a seasoned professional, together we'll peek behind the real estate curtain to help you have a better grasp on what the process entails so you can avoid buying into these misleading marketing messages.

I've developed a passion for helping people, and I have a soft spot for the real estate industry that grew from the beautiful opportunity I've had working with the Buffini & Company organization—a real estate coaching and training company whose mission is to impact and improve the lives of others—since 2006, which has helped me develop my business and gain a deeper understanding of the impact our industry has on the consumer. Therefore, I want to make sure you understand the value of an agent and how to recognize a professional. If you're considering buying or selling a home, you should have someone who you trust and who can be transparent with you helping you through the process.

I live and breathe the principals I'm about to share, and I see them being carried out by many of my co-workers, whom I respect and am thankful for, being living proof that professionalism in our industry can and should be a minimum standard.

Real estate has long been seen as a sales industry, but I believe through and through that I am not a traditional sales person, and that the quality agents in our industry are not old-school salespeople, but are valued, trusted advisors; and my hope is that, as I take you behind the scenes, you'll catch a glimpse of why I hold this truth so close to my heart.

CHAPTER 1

EMOTIONAL INTELLIGENCE–NOT ARTIFICIAL INTELLIGENCE

Helping a buyer or seller with their real estate transaction requires a professional agent to use extensive skills of emotional intelligence. When used properly, these skills can foster a great connection between the consumer and the agent, bringing about calm and ease. On the other hand, an agent poorly skilled in this area can turn a potentially challenging situation into a nightmare.

To be honest, I'd never even heard the term "emotional intelligence" until 2015, when I was at a real estate conference and the book *Emotional Intelligence* by Daniel Goleman was recommended by Joe Niego—often recognized as the best listing agent in America—when discussing the keys to success in real estate—one of which was the possession of emotional intelligence. At another conference, Dr. Henry Cloud, author of the book *Boundaries*, talked about self-awareness and emotional intelligence in leadership. My eyes widened as I started to make the connection between this concept, how it has influenced my success in real estate, and why it matters to the consumer.

Emotional intelligence has many layers, but in a nutshell, it's the ability to monitor your and other people's emotions, identify them appropriately, and use that understanding to guide your thinking and behavior about things that are happening. It's about being able to handle your personal impulses and softening your ego so you don't always have to be right. It is about having grit through difficult situations and the courage to do the right thing. And it's about being able to handle pressure and stress from complicated and uncertain situations.

I know how stressful buying or selling a home can be (doubly so if you're doing both simultaneously, and triply so if you're buying and/or selling out of the area!). It can be an emotional process. For sellers, from the time the home goes on the market and is under contract, to the time the closings finally happen, there's so much uncertainty. And for buyers, it's a rude awakening to learn that the process isn't as perfect as you might have expected. A great real estate agent understands these emotions, can alleviate some of the stress by providing perspective into the process, and can help a client understand what to expect.

Agents who have strong emotional intelligence skills are self-aware, have enough self-control to not bring their own drama into the situation, and know how to empathize with the client about what they're going through. They should also have the self-confidence to stay positive and encouraging and get through common obstacles.

Let's take a look at the case study of the Frank family, homebuyers whom I've worked with a couple of times, to see how both the couple's and my own emotional intelligence successfully integrated into their home-buying process.

CASE STUDY 1: THE FRANK FAMILY

When Eric and Katie Frank needed to find the perfect home for their young family, they knew they wanted more than an average, sales-driven realtor. So when their family referred me with enthusiasm, they reached out to discuss buying a new home. As soon as I met them, it was clear they wanted a realtor who understood the concerns and anxiety that can accompany the process of committing to a six-figure investment. My goal was to set their minds at ease.

When I met with Katie and Eric for the buyers' consultation, I was especially careful to not only detail the buying process from beginning to end, but also to listen closely to their needs, ask empathetic questions, and build a relationship with them. I took the time to get to know them as a family, understand their needs, and use my emotional intelligence skills and expertise to build a relationship of trust with them. My desire to build trust, listen, and be transparent and honest with the Frank family is what enabled me to help them navigate the stress and emotions of the process.

After our initial conversations, it was clear that they were interested in a competitive area where homes were often under contract within a day after being listed. It was my knowledge and intuition that allowed the Frank family to find and secure the perfect home, guiding them through the various options to make a calm, informed decision. This was a very exciting time for them, and I was keenly aware of the emotions they were experiencing, so I wanted to make sure they were well taken care of. This particular situation was complicated though, because my husband and I had planned a trip of a lifetime for our twenty-year wedding anniversary and we were heading out of town. In the midst of trying to figure out how to work with the Frank family while being away, something horrible happened: right before the trip, my father unexpectedly passed away. Being stuck in the juxtaposition between a time of sorrow and a time of joy was complicated, and I struggled to identify the best way to handle the situation. I shared my personal challenges with the Frank family, yet it was important to me that I maintain my professionalism. By having strong emotional intelligence, I was able to monitor my own emotions and remain keenly aware of theirs while navigating the process with skill and care.

When the Frank family found a home during this sensitive time, I remained in close contact, overseeing every step of the process and staying focused on delivering a hallmark customer experience. Knowing that my personal situation and availability could be concerning to them, I made sure they were not neglected. This kind of committed avail-ability was a key factor in easing the stresses they were experiencing. Because long-term relationships are more important to me than any one sale, I've always maintained my friendships and professional relationships. The Frank family was no different. Since the birth of their second daughter, they've sought my help again, this time to sell their home and buy a larger one where they can raise their family. I know that leaving the home they love has been emotional, but I am always here to provide support and help make the process as worry-free as possible. Being able to provide a compassionate yet realistic approach has made all the difference.

Of her experience, Katie says she "believes that it's Wendy's empathetic drive to align her personal and professional integrity that allows her to build lasting relationships with her clients. Wendy has amazing intuition and judgement. Everything she said would happen did happen. She treats her job like a craft and brings her strong personal ethics to work as an agent. That's what took away the fear and worry for us. That's what made all the difference. Wendy never tries to sell us just a house. She always tries to help us find a home."

Despite my personal challenges during the Frank family's buying process, and despite the inherent stress on the Frank family from buying a home, because of our emotional intelligence and communication skills we were able to find them the home of their dreams, not once but twice.

Emotional Intelligence and the Selling Process

Unfortunately, things don't always go so smoothly. I've found in my years of experience that challenges with emotional intelligence skills are usually revealed when agents and sellers begin to discuss pricing. Often, there's a relational friction during the pricing tug-of-war—the back-and-forth over what a seller feels their home should be worth versus what an agent's research and data suggests. Pricing a home can be a statistical and analytical process, but because buying and selling a home has a highly emotional component, too, sometimes certain things can't be quantified. It's not unusual for a seller to feel their home should be worth more due to X, Y, or Z reasons. And they're not entirely incorrect, because sometimes, these unquantifiable emotions do play a role in what a buyer is willing to pay. But more commonly, an agent has to help the seller see that it's not always a good pricing strategy to base price off an unknown, ideal buyer who would be willing to pay more for X, Y, or Z, but, instead, to price more accurately to what an average buyer will pay—if the seller wants to increase their odds of selling in a timely manner.

Sometimes, when a seller doesn't value what a professional agent says, the agent can feel an emotional sting, especially if he or she is confident in their pricing analysis. In these cases, it's easy for an agent to feel devalued as a professional and let those emotions cloud the discussion. It takes strong emotional intelligence to not take this type of conversation personally. On the reverse, the seller may feel emotional about how the market does or doesn't value the cherished features of their home. They may feel insulted or frustrated with the person delivering the news. It takes strong emotional intelligence skills for the agent to understand what the seller could be going through and not take the conversation or frustration personally, but, instead, do their best to guide the seller toward making a good pricing decision. And if for some reason a good decision is not made, the agent should be present to walk the seller through the emotions commonly experienced when the market does not respond favorably.

It's not uncommon for a seller to feel the emotions of loss when their home is rejected by the market. Denial is often the first and most powerful emotion that sellers feel, and agents must be able to identify and help guide them through it. If the seller chooses to blame the agent for the market response, they may often feel angry toward them. Subsequently, frustration often results as a seller moves through the stages of grief and loss, when the value they had hoped to gain from the sale doesn't seem likely. The seller often will find themselves asking for unreasonable things, or blaming the agent during this stage, but an emotionally intelligent agent knows that the frustration, though it may feel like it's directed at them, is ultimately the result of the market response—and the agent is simply seen as the front line to that market. Eventually, disappointment will take hold as the seller begins to realize that maybe the market has not and will not respond to what they'd hoped, and finally, they'll come to accept what needs to be done, if they still want to sell. An agent with emotional intelligence skills will recognize these stages, be understanding and gentle, not take them personally, and, ultimately, continue to guide the seller into making adjustments that will accomplish the end goal of selling the home.

> *An agent with emotional intelligence skills will recognize these stages, be understanding and gentle, not take them personally, and, ultimately, continue to guide the seller into making adjustments that will accomplish the end goal of selling the home.*

Emotional Intelligence and Inspections

Another example where emotional intelligence is commonly required is during the home inspection process, where buyers and sellers can sometimes be at odds with how to interpret the results, and their judgment can be clouded by emotions. Many times, there is a third emotional component to the inspection process: the home inspector. A good one will know how not to heat up the conversation by being overly dramatic about findings. An emotionally intelligent agent can help set expectations of the process and help guide either the buyer or the seller though this sometimes-sensitive next step of the contract.

For example, every house has something wrong with it. Even new construction homes. Houses are built by humans, and even when they're well-maintained, it's almost impossible for owners to know everything that's going on with theirs. So, unless the seller is inspecting their home as an inspector would, it's almost inevitable that things will be found that the seller didn't even know about. Sadly, what often happens in those cases is that the buyer may present a request for minor or insignificant repairs (from the seller's perspective, anyway), making the seller feel insulted and offended. An emotionally intelligent agent will be able to keep the seller calm during this process by explaining the options and how to handle the situation in a pragmatic way. Offering options and suggestions, getting clear on the request and the costs, and, ultimately, helping the seller find a non-emotional response to help the process continue forward are all signs of an emotionally intelligent agent. If all parties stay matter-of-fact in the process and avoid taking things personally, even an unrealistic buyer request can often lead to a favorable compromise. An emotionally intelligent agent will help the owner see both perspectives without adding to the drama. When representing a seller, a good agent will communicate with the buyer's agent to find out what is critical to the buyer, help the seller to understand the buyer's concerns, and encourage them not to take results or requests personally.

Some buyers use the inspection process to renegotiate terms, which can be problematic. But if several issues are unveiled during an inspection, it's not unusual for buyers to grow nervous, which is normal because they don't really have a perspective of what's typical. A mediocre agent is more of an order taker. When representing the buyer, they'll get the inspection report and send it to the seller, asking them to fix everything. But a good agent will help a buyer understand what's important and what's possible to easily handle later. This reassurance and guidance keeps the process moving smoother. An emotionally intelligent agent will know that buying a home is a big deal to the buyer, and that it's important they don't feel they're purchasing a home that may prove problematic later, but at the same time, they'll be able to offer a realistic perspective to the buyer without being an alarmist.

> *An emotionally intelligent agent will know that buying a home is a big deal to the buyer, and that it's important they don't feel they're purchasing a home that may prove problematic later, but at the same time, they'll be able to offer a realistic perspective to the buyer without being an alarmist.*

Emotional Intelligence and Stress

Another critical component of emotional intelligence is being able to resolve conflicts under stressful circumstances. I once had a customer who, on closing day, two hours before signing, took down pictures from the walls and decided to do touch ups on the little holes (which they weren't required to do, but did because they wanted to turn over the house especially nice). As they were touching up, using the right shade of lime green paint, they accidently knocked the can onto the carpet. You can imagine the panic and frustration that ensued. My role was to not take their stress and anger personally, but rather to help them remain calm and offer solutions. Obviously, it wasn't an ideal situation, but we were able to find a solution to satisfy both parties quickly and remain composed during the challenging time. A good agent reassures their clients that, together, you'll get through the challenge and stay on the solution side. That's what I often find myself repeating to clients, "Let's get on the solution side of the problem."

Empathy is probably the number-one emotional intelligence skill a top agent brings to the table. Empathy is not sympathy, which is more like pity or sorrow for someone else. Instead, empathy is an understanding of what is going on with the other person. We often find we have to counsel our clients and comfort them when they see trouble ahead. Understand that buying or selling a home is a big deal to them, don't make light of their concerns, and, instead, offer comfort and share past experiences to reassure them that the agent has done this previously and made it through similar or worse. Offer hope that it will all work out. Guide them through the process and help them get through it. We can't alleviate all stress and uncertainty, but we can be there for our clients and let them know we're partners throughout the process, ultimately guiding them to a better, calmer state of mind.

An agent with strong emotional intelligence builds a connection with clients and gains trust by listening, being transparent, and being honest. Consumers are exposed to tons of data through technology, from family and friends, or even just by watching HGTV. And though they have more information than ever before, it's essential for the agent you work with to connect with you, help you make wise decisions, and navigate the emotions of the process to accomplish what's best for your goals.

Contrary to what many might believe, a good real estate agent does more than just sell homes. Your agent should be more of a professional advisor than a salivating salesperson. They should listen to you and understand what you're experiencing before helping you to navigate the emotional and stressful challenges of the real estate process. That's why I believe emotional intelligence is one of the key characteristics of the best agents in the business.

I think we can all agree that as much as technology's influence has increased in the buying and selling of homes, the real estate buying and selling process includes many emotional aspects that can often derail the transaction—or worse, cause opposing sides to hate (I know, strong word, but I've seen it!) each other. I've even seen clients who don't want to meet for closing because of the emotional stress they've experienced in dealing with the other side. A great agent will always try to help them see the big picture and work toward a solution. Technology and mediocre agents just don't have this skill or ability.

Key Emotional Intelligence Behaviors

So how do you know you have found an agent with emotional intelligence? According to emotional intelligence experts, there are key behaviors to look for. To start, authenticity is an important consideration. Does the agent have positive interactions with you that feel real, open, and honest? Or does the experience come across as scripted and forced? Agents need to be professional in their client dealings, but they also need to be authentic and carry real conversations with a positive attitude.

Confidence and flexibility are other traits to look for. Real estate often has unexpected twists and turns, which means agents should be confident in their approach, flexible in staying the course, and resilient through difficult situations, especially if the difficulty stems from dealing with clients' emotions. These are signs of an agent who can manage and regulate their own behavior in the face of drama.

Lastly, agents should have empathy. They should think about your feelings (versus discounting them), understand your challenges and frustrations, and help you develop a positive and productive perspective toward achieving your goals. If you have an agent who can do the above, congratulations—this means you've found one who has at least one of the seven key characteristics of a pro!

—— *Key Lessons:* ———————————

1. Buying and selling real estate has an emotional component that technology cannot change or simplify.

2. If you work with less-skilled agents or discounted services, it's likely that if/when things go wrong, the situation may become unresolvable due to lack of emotional intelligence these lesser-qualified resources may possess.

3. Working with an agent who has strong emotional intelligence will give you confidence that any bumps or challenges encountered along the way will be navigated with more ease.

CHAPTER 2

CUSTOM SOLUTIONS– CREATING A STRATEGY FOR SUCCESS

Change is the one thing we can always count on. In real estate, that could mean changing where you live, changes in your personal life that affect where you live, or dealing with market changes. Whatever the change, having an agent who can analyze the situation and find a professional solution tailored to your specific needs, in addition to managing change effectively, is what makes all the difference—and that's exactly what a skilled professional offers.

might ruffle a few feathers in this chapter. Mostly because I know many (myself included) have misinterpreted the word I'm about to mention for many years, making incorrect decisions and choices based on its perceived meaning. Today, I hope to bring clarity to this word that I feel is misunderstood, misjudged, and typically frowned upon: sales.

Growing up, I remember being fascinated with real estate. Initially, I wanted to be an architect. I'd sketch dream houses with bowling alleys, multi-level entertainment spaces, and interior gardens (yes, this was the 1980s). However, the college I received a scholarship for didn't offer a degree in architecture, so I chose to study statistics instead since I was good at math ... but I digress.

During my college years, I'd sneak into nearby high-end new construction neighborhoods on Sundays (shh, don't tell anyone), because that's the day the contractors would be off. I'd wander through framed-up mansions, admiring their layouts. Occasionally, I'd run into a homeowner, inspecting the progress of their home, and gush to them about how awesome their new home was going to be. At the time, I didn't think much of the fact that my eighteen- or nineteen-year-old mind was fascinated with new construction while the rest of my girlfriends were busy hitting up the mall or going to the beach. Now I see that destiny or fate may have had a hand in this early interest ... but, again, I digress.

The point is, I remember someone telling me, "You should get into real estate sales," and I thought, "No way! I could never be a sales person." Because of that darned word, "sales," I believed real estate agents convinced people to buy or sell a home when they really didn't want to. That's why my skin crawls a little when our profession is referred to as "salesy."

Of course, I've since learned that real estate sales is not "sales" in the way that word is often interpreted. I don't sell a buyer a house; I give them advice on how to buy it. I don't sell a seller's home; I help a seller position it best and expose it to the market so a buyer will hopefully want to buy it. I provide guidance to help people make informed decisions. Many people mistake sales to mean forcing someone to do something they don't want to, and professional real estate agents don't and shouldn't force or strong-arm someone into doing anything.

I'll give a nod to the *Merriam-Webster's* definition of "sales": "operations and activities involved in promoting and selling goods or services."[1] To that end, a real estate agent "sells" property through promotion and marketing, which we'll cover more in chapter 3. But promoting and marketing are just services—not necessarily the thing selling the home. Sure, an agent can promote a property to a buyer, but no amount of marketing and promotion is going to change a buyer's mind if they don't like the home.

> *I don't sell a buyer a house; I give them advice on how to buy it. I don't sell a seller's home; I help a seller position it best and expose it to the market so a buyer will hopefully want to buy it. I provide guidance to help people make informed decisions.*

So, with my youthful definition of "sales" meaning to force someone to do something, the reality is that sales are much more about promotion, either of a property or of the services provided. But ultimately, I still feel that selling is not what most agents do or what should define a professional real estate agent. It is a small piece, and less critical, of some of our other, more important responsibilities.

---

1   *Merriam-Webster, s.v. "sale (n. pl.)," accessed December 2018, https://www.merriam-webster.com/dictionary/sale.*

Yet, often our industry gets lumped into the sales category.

Solutions, Not Sales

Professional real estate agents are more like service providers who lay out solutions versus those who sell people something they don't want. Real estate involves much more than simply listing and selling homes. A great agent focuses on understanding each client's situation and making sure the solution is a right fit for them as a whole. Offering ideas, options, and solutions, even if they're not what the client wants to hear, are part of a good real estate agent's job description.

For example, many sellers don't want to hear that their home needs a deep cleaning, or a paint touch up, or new carpet, or that the tile they spent four Saturdays installing is so dated that it will turn off most buyers. And most buyers don't want to hear that what they're looking for may not exist, or that they need to adjust their price range or location to get the home they want.

Take, for example, the case study of the Weinberg family, a couple whom I helped over a period of almost two decades—that's right, decades—to finally buy their dream home amid budget constraints, their "must-haves," and the ever-changing markets.

CASE STUDY 2: THE WEINBERG FAMILY

In 2002, I helped Troy Weinberg buy his first home. He was a single man in an up-and-coming professional career. We knew he was looking for something low-maintenance that he could possibly turn into a rental property in the future. Navigating his options at that time was part of the professional solution we discussed. Eventually, Troy decided on a condo in the middle of town.

Years later, after he got married, we connected again, and I helped him and his wife, Jenny, find their first home together.

The family circumstances were different this time around. Buying this home was a big decision for the both of them, and we had to find a solution that would work a bit outside of the box—because it was then 2008, inventory levels were high, and tons of homes were on the market. The professional solution I proposed was to implement a process-of-elimination approach, versus one where they'd select just one option. In no time, the Weinberg family found a home they felt was perfect and met all their needs—and they were able to snag it for quite a bit under asking price.

Fast forward to 2014: The Weinberg family was planning on baby number three, and I was thrilled to be on board again, even though I knew I had a tight timeline to help them both sell and move. Their eldest son was about to start kindergarten, and they had decided on changing school districts by the beginning of the new school year.

Knowing they had a house full of children, toys, and personal effects, I had to provide advice and professional solutions to help them sell—quick. When they seemed overwhelmed with where to store things as they decluttered, I advised them to pack the garage; as long as the inside was "show ready," most buyers could overlook a stuffed garage.

The other challenge we had to navigate through was buying and selling simultaneously in an active market and a top-rated school district. Being sensitive to their goals, timeframe, and market conditions, we came up with a strategy and decided to put their home on the market, since they had to sell before they could buy. We anticipated a quick sale and high demand, and planned to negotiate a contingency to allow the Weinberg family to identify their next home without completely committing to the sale, in case they encountered hurdles finding their next home.

After only one day on the market, their home sold, so we had exactly one week to find a new home and complete the purchase agreement. Jenny Weinberg was more than pleased with the results from the start of her interactions with me.

"You listen," she told me, "and you don't have a cookie-cutter approach. We were not sure where we wanted to be, and you shifted our mind-set to be open to a neighborhood we hadn't considered. You came up with an efficient plan that really was all about timing, so we knew exactly what needed to happen to get us where we wanted to be. And we did it! It all happened quickly. Listing, selling, finding a new home, and closing on the new house, just in time for school to start."

Although they loved the new home they ended up purchasing, the Weinberg family had always dreamed of living closer to the beach—so that was in the back of their mind as a long-term goal. Over the years, we spent time strategizing on how they could make this dream a reality. They'd watch homes come and go on the market, but finding one within their budget proved a challenge. Their desired location was unique, in high demand, and pricey. This time though, the first part of the solution was to determine if they needed to sell to buy. Typically, the homes that fit their needs were limited in number and sold quickly, putting them at risk of trying to sell their home, which could happen quickly without finding the right one to buy, leaving them homeless and having to find an interim home.

As time passed, Jenny spotted a home that she loved, and luckily the lender could qualify them without the need for them to sell. We knew we had to drop everything to see it right away. We made an offer, but multiple offers followed. It was clear to me that we'd have to offer over asking price. The Weinberg family would have to be extremely aggressive, but they were in a good financial position to take action. They were concerned about going overboard, but, knowing what they wanted, I was confident that our approach was the right one. Thankfully, it all worked out on the buying side.

However, the timing on the selling side wasn't so ideal. In all transparency, when brain-storming the solution and pricing strategy, I thought it would all work seamlessly, as their home was in a highly sought-after neighborhood, and they had a lot of great features that the market was hot for. Unfor-tunately, the market grew soft right around the time we entered, which isn't something we could have predicted. There was also a general sentiment among buyers: they preferred homes in newer communities in the area. These communities attracted many buyers, making it difficult to find a buyer who valued what we had to offer. This meant one thing: we had to adjust our selling strategy. Although this wasn't ideal and more than a little unexpected, we had no choice but to come up with a plan to deal with the unusual circumstances, using intuition and observation to find success. It was painful to watch the showings happen while we continued to receive feedback that the buyers would go elsewhere. After some time, we had to regroup and come up with a new plan. We made some investment to the condition of the home and made some staging decisions, emptying rooms, etc., and soon we had a buyer who was mildly-interested. It was the third mildly-interested buyer since the house went on the market, but this time, we were not going to let them get away. We came up with a creative approach to attract the buyer with incentives, and before we knew it we were negotiating a contract. It was a difficult negotiation, but ultimately resulted in the Weinberg family getting the home under contract and closure to their home sale.

As you can see, over the years the Weinberg family's situation evolved, and so did their real estate challenges. Flexibility and out-of-the-box thinking helped me find professional solutions to meet their changing needs. As market and clients' needs change, I find there are different solutions for different scenarios. And it takes listening, strategizing, and being creative to come up with the right mix of professional solutions to see a successful outcome.

Be mindful that many unskilled agents will tell you what you want to hear, not what you need to hear. That approach often leads to discouragement, disappointment, and difficulties during the buying or selling process.

Using a solutions-based approach, however, allows agents to customize a solution for each individual client instead of attempting a one-size-fits-all solution. This model shows clients that we care about their needs as individuals and emphasizes that we see the client as more than just a one-time transaction.

Watch Out

The truth is that it's easy to get a real estate license, which is why so many people do. And the consumer typically knows more than one agent. Or they may go online and find an agent through an ad or discount site. Another problem is that many licensed agents are non-practicing, part-time licensees (which is a whole different topic for another day). But, the bottom line is that there are many agents out there who aren't professional service providers, which is why it's so important to know what makes a great agent.

Because of the ease of entry and their part-time dynamic, when these agents have an opportunity to make money, that becomes their sole focus, versus developing a relationship and providing long-term professional services and solutions. Could you imagine having surgery performed by a part-time doctor or having a part-time attorney represent you? Many consumers don't see the value of hiring an agent, because the ones they know aren't professionals. So they miss out on the services and value a skilled, full-time agent provides.

In order to navigate a salesperson versus a professional services provider, consumers should realize something very important: real estate agents don't get paid until a sale closes. Why should this matter to you? Because this type of compensation structure employed in this profession means that a real estate agent must successfully do their job before they see the light of a paycheck. This structure is why it's easy for lesser-skilled agents or agents with a transactional mind-set to slip into the "chase the commission" mind-set.

Holistic Approach

A professional agent will focus first on building a relationship with you to help you—not on the money. They'll look at the holistic relationship and strive to offer a professional service.

Another way to know you have a great agent is if they provide consultations, not presentations. Many agents, historically, have been taught to give a "sales presentation," which takes us back to that word again: sales. This old-school real estate presentation model promoted techniques for agents to get clients to sign on the dotted line, a lot like time-share presentations, where salespeople are taught to "close" the deal.

A professional services real estate agent, however, will take a more consultative approach. They'll ask questions, get to the bottom of the client's situation, discuss solution options, consult with the client, and give advice and guidance for the best possible solution, all while putting their own self-interests aside.

> *A professional services real estate agent will ask questions, get to the bottom of the client's situation, discuss solution options, consult with the client, and give advice and guidance for the best possible solution, all while putting their own self-interests aside.*

I cannot emphasize enough just how important it is to find a real estate agent who provides professional services, not sales. I've learned that I don't "sell" anything. I strategize and analyze and come up with solutions for my clients' needs. And even if they do end up signing on the dotted line, if they ever felt like they'd made a mistake, I'd graciously see what I could do to help them undo it. Ultimately, that's what anyone who cares about their clients does, beyond just what a transactional agent would do.

—— *Key Lessons:* ————————

1. The word "sales" is often associated with real estate agents, but it has been misunderstood and misapplied to the industry as a whole, based on misinterpretations about what real estate agents actually do.

2. A professional real estate agent is not a salesperson who does presentations and uses tactics to persuade; instead, they consult with clients by listening to their unique situations and laying out customized solutions and options.

3. A skilled and professional agent will not focus on the commission; instead, they'll focus on building a relationship with you.

CHAPTER 3

ANALYSIS AND PROMOTION–POSITION YOURSELF TO WIN

Having confidence that your agent is recommending things that are in your best interest is important. However, when you're selling a home, it can get a bit more complicated, because there's a difference between what a home is worth from an appraiser's and the market's stand point versus what you may think it's worth, and when an agent suggests something unexpected, it can sometimes confuse sellers into questioning where the agent's interests lie. For instance, in an appreciating market, it may be difficult to prove an increased home value. In a depreciating market, old prices may no longer reflect the current market value. A professional agent should provide you with a detailed analysis as well as a comprehensive marketing plan to expose the home to as many interested buyers as possible.

Once the home is buyer ready, a professional agent will work on exposing it to the marketplace. By my previous comments, you might think that I'm pretty opposed to technology, but to be honest, technology helps agents—good, well-intentioned agents—do that job even better; so technology is not so much a disruptor as it is a tool that supports the real estate business. What's interesting is that "in the old days" before technology, the consumer looked to their agent to "find" a buyer for their home and "sell" to them. Occasionally, that still happens. In fact, there's nothing more exciting than working with a buyer who happens to be the perfect match for my seller's home. However, with technology around, having agents source buyers for sellers they represent is an outdated mind-set. The reality is, technology exposes sellers' properties to the consumer a million times better than we ever could without it.

In fact, to me, one of technology's best features is that it arms consumers and agents with more information than ever before. Of course, if not using a reliable source, the accuracy of that information is up for debate. For example, sometimes these sites have homes listed as "foreclosures," yet they aren't really a foreclosure for sale. What's displayed is the public record data of *lis pendens* filings, giving the bank the *right* to foreclose if they so choose. However, the homeowner could work out something with them to resolve the situation, meaning technically the home isn't a true foreclosure for sale the way the listing may indicate. Another example is when data used to generate online valuations does not reflect important factors, such as upgrades or the condition of the property. Or when homes that appear for sale may already be under contract. Or, my favorite, when an owner lists their home online and sets an unrealistic price, skewing perceptions of its true value. But, using a reliable source—like our board of realtors' multiple listing service—where the data has broker accountability and reliable sourcing through professionals' input, arms the agent and consumer with much of what is needed to analyze the market.

In addition, technology provides invaluable resources when it comes to exposing a home to a much larger audience. Online resources help the consumer learn what's for sale, where it's located, what it's priced at, how many days it's been on the market, etc. One of the things technology can't do is build relationships or care about your needs and goals, but for marketing purposes, it's great.

In the following case study on the Reiger family, you can see an example of how technology can be leveraged to both educate and assist you on your journey to selling and buying a home.

CASE STUDY 3: THE RIEGER FAMILY

Marketing and pricing a home can often be an emotional as well as a strategic process. This was especially true after the market crash of 2008, when Bill and Susan Rieger decided to transition from a condo into a single-family home. At that time, the general sentiment was "nothing is selling." And that was the truth, because most people were listing their homes for sale based on what they thought the market should bear, not based on data. It's difficult to price a home correctly, particularly when the market is dropping and there aren't many sales to draw numbers from. I had to analyze the few sales that were happening, make inferences based on what had sold in the past and what had sold recently in the area, and compare that information to the statistical data over the past year.

When the Rieger family asked me to come up with market comparison sale data for their condo, I had to deliver some disappointing news: it wasn't worth quite as much as they'd hoped. As a professional, I strive to provide a sound pricing strategy—that's the key to success—even though, often, the news isn't what I want to share or what my clients want to hear. The important thing is to provide a level of detail that clearly explains how I analyzed the data to arrive at my conclusions and pricing recommendation.

The Reiger family and I had to look at the entire picture, not just what we wanted from the sale but also how it would affect them in buying their next home. They were able to see that, even though the numbers were not what they expected, it was still possible for them to make the move.

After we came to an agreement about how to price their home, we executed on a complete marketing plan. We made a list of actions necessary to get the home ready, hired a professional photographer, made sure the description was compelling, and ensured that the photos were flawless. We were also able to market to agents in the area and adjust our strategy to feedback and market conditions.

The condo sold, and we were able to move on to the next step. I helped the Rieger family find a new home, leveraging data and strategy to help them make an appropriate offer. A few years later, I also helped them purchase a rental property. In both cases, using data to support our offer position helped us accomplish our buying goals.

When the Rieger family decided to make another move almost ten years later, the market had radically shifted. This time, houses were selling quickly, and a home they felt would be perfect for them came on the market. I analyzed market conditions and data and advised them to make a full-price offer on the property, especially as the offer would be contingent on the sale of their current home, which wasn't yet on the market. We communicated to the sellers how we planned to use data to price the Reiger family's home aggressively, which would mean we would sell quickly. They agreed to give us a short time to get the home sold, even though theirs had been on the market only a few days. Providing this in-depth marketing plan and statistical detail gave them confidence that we could get the job done.

When the Rieger family's home sold over asking price in one week, I was also able to negotiate a rent-free month to accommodate their family as they transitioned to their new home. Ultimately, when a seller is looking to make a move, it's easy to get caught up in the emotions of what they feel their home should be worth. Working with the Rieger family was a joy, because they appreciated both the level of detail I provided in the form of industry statistics and my analytical approach to pricing. They also knew that, ultimately, my goal was to understand their needs, tell the truth in love, and price and market their home for a successful outcome.

Of their experience, Bill says, "You helped reset our expectations based on reality, and took us through the process of how to handle a multi-offer environment—which was very, very helpful—and you always understood where the market was and used data to drive our decisions."

Susan agrees: "You helped us see we might not get the value we hoped on this sale, but that didn't mean we wouldn't get it on the next. But it wasn't just about real estate. You asked about life goals. That helped us make good decisions about the market, too."

So you can see how, from a real estate agent's perspective, technology is one of my favorite analysis and marketing tools. However, it requires skill to leverage technology for those purposes, and when someone considers using a real estate agent, they need to make sure that agent is highly skilled with both technology and traditional marketing.

Think of your real estate agent as your personal marketing genie. Marketing has a lot of different elements that only a really great agent will know how to implement for your benefit. Most people think of marketing as getting information about a home in the marketplace. However, a great agent will know that successfully selling a property starts with having a solid understanding of the Home Selling Triangle:

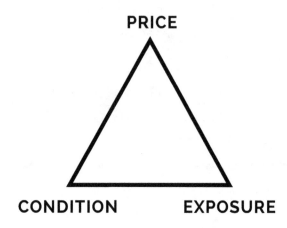

We will discuss each of the three components of this triangle independently.

Condition

To start, a great agent knows that marketing begins with the home's condition. Condition will affect so many things, including how the home shows in person, in photographs, and how a buyer perceives the space.

In-Person Condition

The agent will explain to the seller the importance of looking at the property from the buyer's perspective. Sellers and agents should focus on four key areas:

1. Tiding up the house and storing away personal items that aren't needed.

2. Cleaning the house so the buyer feels the home is well cared for. This includes a deep cleaning of baseboards, flooring, windows, AC systems and vents, cabinets, showers, baths, and toilets, etc.

3. Fixing minor repairs that are distracting and would make a buyer devalue the home.

4. Using aromatic and visual enhancements, such as candles, air fresheners, plants, doormats, decorative towels and accessories, and decorative pillows.

Being able to make specific suggestions to a seller is key. Also having real conversations on how best to handle things that may be sensitive to discuss but are important to merchandise the house.

Online Condition Perception

Next, a good agent recognizes that a home's condition matters not only in how well the home shows in person, but also in how it's perceived online. So to maximize showings online, an agent must recognize the extreme importance of professional photography. How many times have you seen an advertised home with no photos, one photo, or blurry or dark photos? It pains me when agents don't understand the importance of quality. My guess is, either they don't have the resources to properly photograph the property or they have no awareness of how a poorly photographed home devalues the perception of its worth in the marketplace—or worse—causes potential buyers to overlook it completely. A researcher at Zillow found that, over a seven-day period, listings with at least one photo were likely to be viewed 41 percent more times than listings with no photos.[2]

It's disheartening to see sellers hire agents who aren't professionals and end up with no photos or repellent images of their home as their first impression to the market. The truth is, most homes' first showings happen online more often than not. So it's imperative that the images entice buyers to come

---

2   Jason Tan, "Click Me! Click Me!" Zillow Porchlight, August 28, 2008, https://www.zillow.com/blog/click-me-click-me-5513/.

see the home in person after the online "showing." Otherwise, the property is likely to be overlooked.

A good real estate agent knows the value of professional photos and should have a relationship with quality real estate photographers who know what's needed to make the home show its best. Additionally, the agent should offer the seller tips on how to prepare their home for photographs, arming them with useful information for getting the home ready.

Bottom line, a knowledgeable agent will know which photos will attract a buyer and arrange them accordingly. In my experience, the average buyer looks through the first five to ten photos before deciding whether or not to continue. If the first five photos are of the front of the house with none of them displaying other rooms that interest buyers (such as kitchens, baths, living rooms, outdoor space, etc.), then the buyer will often move on. Some buyers do get a little frustrated if the photos jump around, but a good agent knows that at least the first five must showcase the home before the rest go in order.

Emotional Condition

Along the same lines as the photographer showcasing the home through images, another aspect of marketing is staging. We touched on this earlier, but getting the home ready starts with basic decluttering (pre-packing, as we like to call it). It also involves arranging furniture and personal items in such a way that appeal to a buyer as they take in their surroundings and walk through the home. For example, grouping furniture in a way that leads the buyer to perceive the room as a quiet, relaxing place, or conversely, as a place to engage in conversation. Putting personal items out that invite a buyer to envision themselves entertaining people, having a glass of wine, or reading a book by the fireplace creates an emotional attachment to the space. Decorative pillows, fluffy towels, flowers, and candles create an emotion of comfort and beauty.

A professional agent will have a real discussion with the seller on the condition and set up of their home, and, if needed, discuss hiring a professional stager (if the agent isn't already certified to be one). There's a difference between staging and decorating, but many people confuse the two. Decorating is designing a home and creating an effect to an individual's liking. Staging is designing a home as if it were a product being merchandised—it's the added "oomph" that makes homes sell faster, and for more money. Understanding buyer psychology and the types of furnishings and effects that most attract buyers are skills that a professional stager can bring to the table.

Although staging is not required, a good agent will be able to explain its significance to sellers and know when to pull in a professional stager, because how we live in and use our homes is different from how we market or merchandise them to the consumer. In fact, any high-ticket item being sold must be presented in a way that attracts customers.

Exposure

Decluttering, cleaning, repairs, staging, and photography are at the top of the list of must-haves for maximixing conditions. However, we can't put all our eggs in those baskets; we must factor in another important part of the marketing triangle that helps to reel buyers in: exposure. The first step to effective exposure is the description. Having a compelling, inviting description elicits a visual experience of emotions, which is what a professional agent should provide. For example, using phrases like "relax on the back porch," or "enjoy your luxury glamour bath," or "witness breathtaking sunrises over the lake," or "appreciate an open and bright floorplan" contain vivid or emotional words and create an experience a buyer can visualize.

Additionally, the description should emphasize things that buyers are interested in: the entry, entertainment space, kitchen, master suite, outdoor space, updates and upgrades, and unique features of the home. A good agent will know what to say and which features to focus on.

To effectively use technology and maximize exposure, an agent must make sure that the home looks outstanding and it is well-described, as it will likely be featured on all major search sites. But what if a buyer isn't actually searching yet? A professional agent will know how to use technology to market the property through social media (both personal and company social media marketing is advised). Currently, social media is one of the biggest and most effective types of online marketing, and a professional agent will know the tools and be active on these mediums with a good volume of friends/followers. Marketing done through these channels (Facebook, Twitter, etc.) should not be "salesy"; instead, it should create excitement about the property. Having a sharable website for individual properties or a link to property details can help the agent, their company, and the owners reach out to their sphere to see if anyone in their networks may have an interested party. Using technology to attract buyers can be a great marketing tool.

Of course, a professional agent won't rely on technology alone to expose the home to the market. An important facet of marketing is peer-to-peer marketing. Having a well-connected agent in the real estate community who can reach out to other agents in their network is a great way to expose the home and gain more interest. Some properties may even benefit from what's known as a "Broker Open." Being familiar with top agents in the area and marketing to them directly can also garner additional exposure. A professional agent will be able to explain to you their peer-to-peer marketing process, such as networking, sharing information with peers in their offices, and/or emailing and mailing other agents in the marketplace.

Finally, the old-school practice of mailing postcards in the neighborhood is actually still common and has been known to effectively generate exposure. Often, neighbors may know someone who might want to buy in the neighborhood, so making them aware of a property that's for sale can be helpful. Open houses can sometimes be useful, though there are a few schools of thought on that. Some people are more conservative and don't want buyers who aren't pre-qualified or don't have an agent who knows them personally traipsing through their home. Open houses do attract more foot traffic from people who aren't serious buyers, such as people who are just looking for the sake of curiosity. However, they can also draw in buyers who have a true interest in the home but whose agents aren't immediately accessible at the moment. Also, there are times when market conditions might warrant an open house less effective. For instance, in a seller's market, open houses are popular because many buyers are selecting from limited inventory. In a buyer's market, there's less urgency for a buyer to rush and see a home, and we find that open houses are less frequented and effective. Bottom line, a professional agent will share pros and cons with their client, consider all factors, and decide if an open house makes sense.

At the end, there are many ways to use technology and traditional marketing to gain exposure for a property. But there's an elephant in the room that must be acknowledged. And although it pains me to say this, you may already know it anyway. So here it goes: no amount of marketing will sell an overpriced home. There. I said it.

> *But there's an elephant in the room that must be acknowledged. And although it pains me to say this, you may already know it anyway. So here it goes: no amount of marketing will sell an over-priced home. There. I said it.*

Price

It's not complicated—99 percent of the best marketing strategies ever invented in the history of real estate play on one simple rule: Price it right. Price is probably the single most effective marketing strategy we have. The natural tendency is to think, "A buyer will just make a different offer if they think the price is too high." In truth, that's possible. But in reality, most buyers feel like it's a waste of their time to make an offer on an overpriced home—just like many sellers feel it's a waste of their time to entertain buyers who don't make a reasonable offer.

Many sellers believe that an overpriced property can be reduced in price if it doesn't sell. A professional agent will warn and educate the seller on the dangers of this type of an approach—by the time the property is finally reduced to a fair market value, it may have been sitting on the market so long that buyers may question it, perceive it to have issues, and possibly make an offer below the actual value to compensate for these doubts.

Instead, knowledgeable agents will provide analytical advice to clients. They'll know how to analyze data so they can provide the seller with options on how to favorably position themselves in the market. A good agent doesn't just give a number, they explain how they arrived at the recommendation by using clear, precise, and predictable data. Pricing is much more than calculating a home's worth based on square footage (another pet peeve I notice with less-skilled agents; this is a rudimentary calculation that fails to effectively factor in the features of the property).

Getting the price right is not an exact science, because no one can predict what any given buyer will be willing to pay for a home. But, as a professional agent, I cringe when I hear, "We just need the right buyer to come along." I agree, we do need the right buyer, but pricing the home right is what will bring in that buyer.

Therefore, a professional agent will analyze the following:

1. **Sold homes.** Recently sold homes provide great data to analyze. These are the homes an appraiser uses to determine value of

other, similar homes in the area—and an appraisal will always be required unless a buyer pays cash for their home. Therefore, sold homes factor high in an estimate. Professional agents should do an analysis that considers more than just price per square foot, instead adjusting for key factors like lot size and view, construction design, amenities, pool, square footage, bedrooms, bath, fireplace, garage, etc.

2. **Pending homes.** Pending home data is typically the most recent data. Whereas sold homes typically consist of contract data at least thirty days prior to the closing date, pending homes are those that haven't yet closed but are likely indicative of accepted contracts within the last thirty days, so we have data to support what asking price generated an offer, which ultimately is what a seller wants. The downside of pending homes is that it's impossible to predict the final price and terms the home will close at, but the data offers an accurate indication of which asking prices generated interest and offers from recent buyers.

3. **Active sales.** What current sellers are asking should play a role in pricing decisions, albeit not as heavily. Sometimes it's even necessary to scope out direct competitors before making a final pricing recommendation. However, regardless of what sellers are asking, it's only pending and sold homes that predictably indicate what most buyers are willing to pay. Active sales are on the "unsold" list, and may be reflective of fantasy and desire, not reality, so they should be weighted less heavily.

4. **Market conditions.** Interest rates, quantity of inventory of homes for sale, the economy, and consumer confidence all influence the sale of a home. Each of these factors is beyond an agent's control, but a professional agent will respond to conditions with the appropriate marketing and price considerations.

And then there's one more factor a good agent will help the seller consider: the ultimate dilemma of pricing.

These dilemmas boil down to three scenarios:

1. you price to market, which means you price fair to increase the likelihood of a sale;

2. you price too aggressively, which means you might leave some money on the table but increase your odds of a sale or possibly multiple offers; or

3. you overprice, which means you can languish on the market without activity.

Price it right and buyers hunting for a great home at a good price will feel they've found that in your home.

Ultimately, the initial asking price should be set by the seller, with recommendations from the agent. I believe price is the number one factor a good agent should help the seller get right, however, a good real estate agent will maximize the seller's home value in the market by knowing the components that influence a sale.

—— *Key Lessons:* ——————————

1. Make sure you're choosing an agent who has a marketing plan, which includes professional photos.

2. The condition of the property is an important leg of the Home Selling Triangle.

3. Pricing a home correctly means considering many facets of data as well as market conditions.

CHAPTER 4

NEGOTIATING WITH EXPERTISE–NO DRAMA!

Negotiation is one of the key skills needed to help clients accomplish their goals. As a real estate agent, I often handle negotiations between buyers and sellers, but also with agents or clients, even often helping couples through negotiations with each other. Many people relate the word "negotiation" with "win-lose," but there's a great deal more to it.

Negotiation. To some, that's a bad word. Most people run from negotiation because they think, "I hate confrontation," or, "I never seem to get what I want." Negotiation has gotten a bad rap over the years, I think, because when most people think about it and about sales, they're reminded of instances where someone attempted to control a sale through a great pitch and sleazy sales tactics that guilted them into signing on the dotted line. Once the ink dries, they experience this sinking feeling, thinking, "Oh my, what in the world did I just agree to?"

Many consumers mistakenly think that if someone is good at negotiating, it means they can make people roll over and say, "Sure, I'll give you what you want."

But that's not what negotiation is all about. In fact, there's a paradigm shift taking place that should influence the way people think about this term, particularly surrounding the difference between old-school and new-school sales.

For example, in old-school sales, the belief was that you were a good salesperson/negotiator if you used a lot of smooth talking to make a pitch. New-school sales is more about asking effective questions to discover each person's needs and presenting solutions to solve challenges. In today's world of abundant information, data, and transparent relationships, negotiation does not have to be salesy.

> **In today's world of abundant information, data, and transparent relationships, negotiation does not have to be salesy.**

Merriam-Webster defines "negotiate" as: "to confer with another so as to arrive at the settlement of some matter"; I particularly like how the definition goes on to state, "Negotiate means to deal with some matter or affair that requires ability for its successful handling and to arrange for or bring about through conference, discussion, and compromise."[3] In real estate speak, this basically translates to two or more ("more" being the key word) people interacting to reach agreement on one or more (again, "more" being the key word) issues. Usually there are more than two people involved in a negotiation between agents, buyers, sellers, etc. Even if two single people are part of a discussion, we're still up to at least three or four people involved when you consider those

---

3   *Merriam-Webster*, s.v. "negotiate (v.)," accessed December 2018, www.merriam-webster.com/dictionary/negotiate.

people to be part of a couple, a family, etc. And usually, there's more than one issue to discuss and come to an agreement on.

In the case of the Holmes family, outlined in the following case study, we ended up experiencing some pretty complicated negotiations that resulted in some setbacks initially, but you'll see how we were prepared for this and ultimately got them what they wanted.

CASE STUDY 4: THE HOLMES FAMILY

When I first had the pleasure of working with Rick and Marianne Holmes, we didn't anticipate just how thoroughly we'd have to master almost all the different negotiation types! What initially seemed like a straightforward process developed into many layers of discussion and key negotiation strategies.

To start with, they'd lived in their beloved custom family beach home for seventeen years but decided to part with it when they realized they wanted to downsize. Understandably, their deep connection to the house led to some mixed feelings on how to price it. We listened to the market and were able to adjust our pricing enough to generate interest, but still, receiving low offers was painful for them.

Through some difficult but deep conversations—between them as a couple, between us as agent and seller, and between agent and buyer—we negotiated a sale they felt good about.

It takes skill to work through all the personalities and issues involved and come to an agreement. We had to work hard to see past the emotional components of the sale and work toward a solution. Then, just when we thought we had it all figured out, repair negotiations seemed ready to derail the situation. The buyer and seller had agreed to an extended period for inspections and a shortened period for response to any repair requests, with the understanding that the buyers would not be nit-picky about repairs due to other favorably agreed upon contract terms. However, when it came time to submit the requests, they delivered a substantial list of repairs without factoring in the average condition of homes the same age as the seller's, which resulted in some heated discussions.

As a skilled negotiator, I knew we had to stay calm and keep perspective. Fortunately, things calmed down and we had a good closing with the buyers, resulting in a peaceful, happy ending. In fact, they've even stayed in contact throughout the years, which speaks highly to the importance of not getting caught up in the heat of emotions, not taking things personally, and understanding that negotiations can bring out a different side of people's personalities that may not be a true depiction of who they normally are—especially in a state of heightened agitation. However, once we come to an agreement and calmness sets in, the process can be very exciting and a happy time for everyone involved.

When Rick and Marianne decided to buy again, they chose a house that was owned by the listing agent, so it was critical to have a very professional negotiation process and get the agent/seller to work toward a positive outcome. The home was extremely unique, with few comparable properties to help us determine our target offer. Many negotiations between agents, as well as between agents and buyers, took place, not only to find the right price, but also to land terms that all parties would consider. The challenge, however, was that there was insufficient data to justify how a price (whether asking price, offer, or counteroffer) was being presented, meaning that these figures often boiled down to how people "felt" like pricing them. Negotiating on feelings is a red flag, but sometimes—particularly without sufficient data to support either side's position—it simply cannot be avoided. We had to find a way through contradictory opinions in order to find middle ground. And fortunately, we had a seller who wanted to sell and a buyer who wanted to buy, and all parties were able to come to an initial agreement.

As negotiations continued, I helped the buyers to address repairs and other issues, customizing my approach to each situation. In negotiations, I've found it's best not to shoot from the hip, and, instead, to slow down, put everything in writing, think through the options, and then send your proposal to the client for review. As we pondered and solidified decisions for each issue, we remained pragmatic and analytical without becoming emotional. This allowed us to anticipate how the other side might respond and accomplish our goals while staying reasonable in our approach.

Working on both these sales allowed us to experience many types of negotiations and develop multiple strategies and approaches to dealing with the unexpected during a very important and emotional process, which brings me to another point: A good negotiator knows how to diffuse the emotion, provide options to consider, guide the client to make informed decisions, and, ultimately, ensure they feel great about the end result.

The best news is they are happy in their new house.

"We had to navigate the unknowns," Rick admits, "and you were like our compass. Emotions kicked in. We pushed back a little on what you were telling us, but you helped us see that give and take is important. It all came together."

From this, it is easy to see how this could become a complicated process, and why a professional agent must know negotiation approaches and techniques to help all parties involved arrive at a successful decision. Unfortunately, when you use online real estate agent sources or discount firms, you'll get agents whose negotiation skills are lacking, or more commonly, agents who are less driven to maximize their client's position because they're not getting paid well to do so. There's very little incentive to really understand the nuances of the process and help clients in the most effective manner possible, in these cases.

Competitive and Collaborative

On the flip side, a professional agent is likely to be more knowledgeable about the varying degrees of competitive or collaborative attitudes. For example, someone who is competitive may see only a win-lose scenario, be overly concerned with their own needs, and will readily sacrifice others' needs to get what they want. They're more interested in controlling the process and using information against the other party than in building trust. On the other hand, someone who is collaborative may work toward a win-win by considering both parties' needs and coming to a mutually satisfying agreement. These people tend to have a give-and-take attitude, which helps build trust and develops respectable relationships. There are also compliant negotiators—people who consider it most important to be accepted and liked, who will sacrifice their own needs to avoid conflict and satisfy the other party. There isn't a right or a wrong way to negotiate. The key is to find an agent who has the skills to facilitate negotiation successfully, regardless of the attitudes involved.

> **There isn't a right or a wrong way to negotiate. The key is to find an agent who has the skills to facilitate negotiation successfully, regardless of the attitudes involved.**

Communication Styles

Also, there are multiple communication styles when it comes to negotiation. Some negotiators are people pleasers who share all their information right off the bat. Others posture, meaning they don't share anything. I've seen both the logical style, where no emotions are involved, and also the reverse—where so many emotional highs and lows are involved, it's hard to know what to expect. I see communication styles where the other person wants to move quickly, or they give up; whereas others work slowly, needing lots of time to digest and think through options. I tend to favor the earnest and honest approach—not giving everything away, but also sharing what's important to my clients and learning what's important to the other side so I can find common ground. A professional agent will recognize the varying styles of negotiation and adjust to accommodate them so success can result.

At the end of the day, with so many details to decide, emotions to consider, data to interpret, and negotiations to navigate, it's amazing that anything ever gets done! Every stage of the process has consequences, so having a skilled agent who knows how to navigate the waters successfully is key.

As we discussed earlier, emotional intelligence is a critical characteristic your real estate agent should have. Part of the reason for this is that minimizing emotions and eliminating negative perceptions during negotiation will help the deal move forward. Once negative emotions enter the discussion, however, trust starts to deteriorate, often driving conversations south. A good agent will work to raise the dialogue from emotional trenches and get on the solution side of the conversation. Because otherwise negotiations can grow competitive, hostile, abusive, or aggressive, and it can be challenging to come to a settlement. I've found that collaboration and a willingness to explore alternative options can often influence the other side to move toward an agreement. Ultimately, that's what negotiation is about—finding a way to settle and agree.

Power

In addition, a good agent will know how to access the power of negotiation—meaning becoming the person with more leverage. As much as I'd like to say negotiations happen on an even playing field, that's rarely the case. Market conditions, the consequences of decisions, and the ability to walk away all play a role in who wields the most power in a negotiation. Having power doesn't necessarily guarantee a win, but it can help tilt the scale during discussions. However, being on either side of power requires skill, too.

For example, one chief power we often see used in negotiations is the power to walk away. He who walks first, wins. Of course, "win" is subjective, but the idea is that if you're a seller, for instance, and you don't have to sell, you hold more power in negotiation. If you're a buyer, it could mean that you don't have to have a particular house—another will do just fine and you can walk away, meaning you have more power in the negotiation. Other power principals include being able to use facts, figures, and logic to support your position. Those often help, but because there's emotion involved in the process too, I've found that it often overshadows logic.

Sometimes, the best skill is to be able to see all perspectives and present options, even if they're not "ideal wins," regardless of who holds the most power.

Tactics

It's also important to know that many tactics can be used in negotiation, and a good agent can not only recognize when they're being used, but also know when to use them. It's sometimes amusing to see how these tactics can play out in discussions. For example, a competitive negotiator may try to use intimidation, short deadlines, or low ball/high ball negotiation to attempt a win. Sometimes it's interesting to watch a competitive negotiator try various tactics to wear down the other side, with marginal success. In today's relationship-based environment, I find that many of these tactics fall flat, whereas a collaborative negotiator may use fairness and trust-building tactics to get what they want. These types of negotiators will ask questions to understand all parties' needs, explore creative options when needed, and communicate in a way that creates positive emotions, encouraging the other party to hopefully cooperate.

Sometimes, we'll come across a client who says, "So, whose side are you on?" That is a shortsighted view of negotiation. Of course, a professional agent's job is to advocate for their client's interest, but it's also important to understand the other party's perspective so we can explore options and determine whether we can work toward a solution.

Ultimately, professional real estate agents should use a balance of assertiveness and cooperation when helping clients approach the negotiation of their real estate transaction. They must protect clients' interests but also feel confident that the other side believes they've received an acceptable outcome, too. Having a less skilled or caring representative could still result in a sale, but be an inadequate experience for all involved.

> *Ultimately, professional real estate agents should use a balance of assertiveness and cooperation when helping clients approach the negotiation of their real estate transaction.*

For example, during a negotiation, a seller may receive a low-ball offer and be tempted to reject it right off. But a professional agent will usually encourage a counter—even if it never goes anywhere—just to keep the conversation going. Often, low offers are equivalent to an emotional insult for the seller, yet some buyers feel the need to at least try with one. It's a normal part of the process, and helping the seller see that perspective is key.

Another one of my most poignant examples of the emotional connection people have when negotiating on their homes are appliances. People are quite often attached to these little buggers! For example, a seller might say, "We're not leaving the refrigerator," and then the buyer enters, and the first thing they see is the refrigerator—what do you think they want now? The refrigerator! The next thing you know, everyone's forgotten about the house and is fighting over a refrigerator (or the washer and dryer, the fountain in the yard, the Jacuzzi … the list can go on). A professional agent knows how to analyze the power in a situation and also offers solutions, such as trades or exchanges, that may defuse the situation and help parties come to a settlement.

Win-Win

Also, a professional knows that win-win doesn't necessarily mean "divide in half" and that the key to a successful negotiation is to find out what's really important to both sides. A professional real estate agent will work toward getting the best price for their clients but also recognize that the terms and options may matter more—and be critical to coming to an agreement. Ultimately, the results of a successful sale matter most, more than any one thing in the discussion.

For example, buyers constantly weigh the value of a home, which is often determined by the benefits they're getting (location, style, etc.) for the price. If the benefits don't outweigh the price, they may not feel inclined to pay the price. Interestingly, many buyers purchase on emotion and then justify by logic. It's imperative that buyers feel connected to the benefits to see value. During negotiations, a professional agent will know how to use the what's-in-it-for-me principle and successfully communicate it to all parties. If needed, they may even exchange/trade items of value to reach an agreement for mutual benefit.

Sometimes, people can be persuaded because they feel a connection to the person on the other side of the discussion. For example, many times sellers will choose to sell to a family "like theirs" over a cash investor who may be turning the home into a rental—even though the latter may be a better deal, the connection between the buyer and seller is an influencing factor.

Finally, people are often persuaded by logical reasoning, and a good agent will be able to present facts logically as to why the parties should come to agreement. The good news is, the market today is very transparent with data, which can easily be used to help position a person's point as valid. But because emotions often win over logic, too much weight here may not always guarantee success. However, data is still one tool that should be considered in the negotiation process.

By now, you know that any agent you choose should have the skills and experience to negotiate like a pro. Too often, a less-skilled negotiator, or even an online source, can serve as just a messenger without delivering options or presenting possible solutions. Instead, a great agent should always help the consumer keep their sights on the end result: helping all parties come to agreement. Finding strategies for success, helping all parties gain perspective, and eliminating emotions to deliver a successful outcome are some of the many key traits an agent should have. Negotiation skills are not just about making the other party do what you want, they're also about giving sound advice, and getting everyone to the finish line.

> *By now, you know that any agent you choose should have the skills and experience to negotiate like a pro.*

Key Lessons:

1. Negotiation is less about getting everything one side wants and more about finding common ground that is mutually satisfying.

2. Hiring a skilled negotiator is one of the key factors in a successful sale.

3. Ultimately, the final result—selling or buying the home—is bigger than the minutiae details that sometimes overpower our thoughts in the moment, blurring the big picture.

CHAPTER 5

SKILLED TRANSACTION MANAGEMENT–SMOOTHING OUT A BUMPY RIDE

Being able to skillfully manage a transaction and guide the consumer through the potential bumps in the road is a key skill that professional agents bring to the table. There are so many things that can (and do!) happen throughout the process, that knowing what to expect, clearly communicating options, and successfully bringing a sale to closing can mean the difference between disaster and a job well done.

So we made it through negotiations and have a signed agreement—whew! And, oh yeah, baby, we're ready to move!

Well, hang on there, cowboy. Just a few more things to get through—and, in fact, this is one of the most important places a true professional adds value to the process: in the middle.

Real estate isn't rocket science—almost anyone can "complete" a real estate transaction without much skill. Even if things often go haywire in the process, the deal can eventually still close. It is no wonder consumers may consider all agents to be the same—because when a sale occurs, albeit managed poorly, the agent is still compensated the same as someone who is very skilled, making it hard to know the difference between a professional agent and an imposter. Ironically, when things are handled well, no one pays attention. It's only when problems arise that we sit up and pay heed.

An important distinction though, is that a professional real estate agent will perform a transaction well. They have the skills, experience, and systems in place to know what needs to happen and which paths to take. They provide a higher level of experience than someone who's just trying to push a sale through to get paid at the end. And although everything may not go perfectly smooth in a transaction, when issues do pop up, a professional real estate agent will know which options to consider and will be able to guide their client through rough situations.

Buying and selling a home is much more involved than simply finding a buyer or seller. Even if the negotiation goes smoothly and no apparent issues arise, the almighty sales contingencies are still on the horizon. A professional real estate agent will provide great value between contract and closing, knowing what needs to happen when and how to navigate the bumps in the road when they occur.

When I worked with the Lushka family, as you'll see in the following case study, my role as an agent was invaluable to them when it came to transactions.

CASE STUDY 5: THE LUSHKA FAMILY

Timothy Lushka and his wife, Katelyn, had been living in an apartment for several years and were a bit uncertain about buying a home. Because of our initial consultation, they felt more confident in what to expect and decided to buy. They quickly found a home they fell for. Little did they know that many challenges were still to come.

The interest rate was on the verge of an uptick, so I enlisted my preferred lender for the Lushka family and secured a last-minute approval. Having a team of referral partners that work with the same level of detail and care of our signature service model is one of the keys to solid transaction management. Knowing what to do when is important, but knowing who to do it with is the power of a solid transaction process.

One of the first steps to most real estate transactions is the inspection. Although most people have an eye for the obvious, getting a professional inspector who specializes on a daily basis in examining the physical details of properties will provide peace of mind to the buyer, and a more-detailed knowledge of the home's condition to all parties involved.

On the day of the inspection, Tim and I arrived at the house to find the inspector waiting for us, which was a little unusual, since the inspector is usually busy checking out the property.

"There's good news and there's bad news," he said. That was an understatement. The first floor of the home was underwater, flooded by a bathroom leak that hadn't been there when we put in our offer. When Tim shared the news with Katelyn, she was heartbroken, certain that this would be a deal breaker. I assured her that although the flooding was major, we could look for a solution, and it could likely be dealt with in negotiation to be repaired by the seller.

One of the challenges of transaction management is knowing that pretty much everything can be worked through, even when the direst of circumstances seem insurmountable. I say "everything" loosely, because there are times when we just know the deal's over. But most of the time, a professional agent skilled in transaction management will be able to access the situation, as unique as it may be, and help all parties to get on the solution side.

As negotiations ensued with the seller on how to handle this unpleasant surprise, I stayed in close contact with the Lushka family. After we reached an agreement, my focus turned to the repairs. Although I'm not a home inspector, I continued to monitor the progress of the repairs, so that once everything was repaired, we could have it all professionally re-inspected.

Since any transaction can get messy, transparency and communication are key. I always understand that though we may not be able to do anything in the moment, being available to talk to clients through their questions and concerns keeps the process running smoother.

With the Lushka family, there were many deadlines to watch, many reminders of "what's next" to account for. We have systems in place for every step of the process so no detail gets missed, no deadline is forgotten, and all parties stay abreast of progress. Sometimes the other side does not fulfill their obligations, and that can be frustrating. But we make sure the client is kept aware of everything that's happening, so there are no surprises. And if out-of-the-norm surprises do pop up, we're quick to take action, stay calm, and find a way to maintain steady progress toward the end result.

By staying open to their needs, cognizant of the terms of the contract, and ready to advise next steps when things went sideways, I was able to help the Lushka family to manage the ups and downs of the process and finally secure the home of their dreams.

"I knew nothing going in," Timothy says. "But I knew you'd be honest with us. You wouldn't sugarcoat the process. At times, it was scary. We had to make a choice to stay or pull out. You supported us in either decision, and gave us the information to make an informed decision. You went to the house several times to supervise, to make sure everyone was doing the right thing and the repairs were done right. If we came up with a question late at night, we knew we'd get an answer from you right away."

Coordinating, watching deadlines, and juggling all the moving parts so things go as smoothly as possible is what a professional agent does. Had I not been there for the Lushka family, things could have gone a lot differently for them. There are many painful stories I could share about clients' encounters with unskilled agents.

Protect Your Money

One example: Once when I was on the listing side of a sale, a buyer was represented by a company who promised to share a portion of their commission with the buyer. The buyer wanted to make an offer—and the agent presented an incomplete one. After getting it all corrected, we still had challenges in negotiating, because the agent was just an order taker who didn't have any skill to explain their client's position to me and my seller, or have the backbone to communicate what was happening and how to best proceed to the buyer. Amazingly, we came to agreement. I was put in a challenging situation because I could see the buyer's agent was making mistakes, but I would not be serving my client well if I pointed them out. One particularly extreme example was the fact that this buyer had a $10,000 binder. In our contracts, the binder is contingent upon inspections, with ten days to either back out, or request repairs. On the twelfth day, the buyer presented an extensive list of outrageous repairs/upgrades that the seller was not inclined to agree to. But because the agent had missed the deadline, the buyer had no remedy. Since they were past the ten-day deadline, they couldn't "cancel" because the seller said no. This buyer almost lost their $10,000 several times throughout the process. Fortunately, I had a calm and even-keeled seller who, though frustrated with the buyer and their agent's mishandling of the process, was reasonable enough to proceed, although he didn't have to. The buyer had delays with financing, which also put their binder at risk. It was through patience and quite a lot of hand-holding that we were able to finalize this sale. Had the seller not been as good hearted, and I had not played stabilizer and brought assurances to the process, the contract would have fallen through and the buyer would have been out $10,000. So in the buyer's effort to use a "cash back" agent, he almost lost more than he would have gained.

This is just one example of the reasons I implore you, dear reader, to make sure you are working with a pro. Because things are going to come up. There are almost always pitfalls in every transaction. A skilled agent has systems in place to watch for them and strategies to overcome them with—here we go again—emotional intelligence and custom solutions. These skills interweave throughout the process.

Something as simple as the binder earnest money deposit not being delivered on time, or even delivered at all, or not being held where it was disclosed to be, can cause a buyer to lose out. Protecting the client's money is a professional's number-one priority. And there are processes, procedures, and rules that must be followed, which many unskilled agents mess up. If not managed carefully, these could cause problems later in the process. When an inspection is done late, or contractual timeframes are not met, that binder earnest money deposit is put at risk. I've seen it more times than I care to admit—consumers who try to save money end up choosing an agent unwisely, costing them more than if they'd hired a professional to begin with.

> *Consumers who try to save money end up choosing an agent unwisely, costing them more than if they'd hired a professional to begin with.*

Inspections, Repairs, Appraisal, Oh My!

The reality is, a real estate transaction is littered with potential snags. We aren't dealing with perfect homes (even new constructions have flaws), as evidenced by the items that spring up on home inspection reports. Of course, home inspectors are paid to find something, and for some reason, the longer their report, the more a client feels they got their money's worth from the inspection. However, these inspections often find little things that aren't material to the livability or functionality of a home, yet can cause a transaction to go sideways. Or they can find big things that need to be addressed, making the situation appear deeply concerning. Knowing when to walk away or stay the course is an important consideration. And feeling confident that you are getting this input from a trusted advisor, and not just someone who is after a commission, is key.

A professional agent knows the best strategies and advice to give clients to get them closer to a successful resolution. Not every situation is "cookie cutter," and a pro will have the knowledge and skill to come up with options and alternatives outside of the box.

As previously mentioned, it's important to educate and provide clear expectations of the home-buying process to clients: what's likely to be found in inspections, what items are customarily addressed, and which ones are minor issues that can be taken care of after closing. You don't want an unskilled agent who just asks for everything on the report to be fixed or who just does whatever the buyer asks without first discussing the nuances together. Honestly addressing the pros and cons of offering a credit in lieu of repairs or using a home warranty are the types of discussions a true professional should have with a client.

Inspections are just one of the many potential difficulties. Most contracts also add appraisal discussions to the mix. In cash transactions, appraisals aren't required, yet the buyer may still choose to include one. However, for financing, at least as of the time this book is being written, lenders require an appraisal. Many potential hiccups around the appraisal process exist; the simplest one being, what if it doesn't appraise? Apart from the obvious concern of a faulty appraisal, there are the more practical, "What do we do next?" questions that often arise that, if handled unprofessionally, can derail the situation.

Another issue I've seen is an appraiser calling for repairs on a home that's being sold as-is. There are plenty of ways to address this issue, and a professional will look at the client's specific situation before offering advice. For example, if an appraiser calls for repairs, a seller could choose to cancel the contract. However, the more likely and preferred scenario is that they'd proceed with some compromise. Often, the repairs will be completed without hassle, but if the repair involves something costly, like installing a new roof, often it can be split between the buyer and seller. Closing costs, or possibly even the contract price, can be renegotiated to accommodate costly repairs required by a lender. I've also seen buyers switch lenders or change to a rehab-type loan product to resolve concerns. Bottom line, these are the type of conversations a professional skilled agent would have with their client and the other parties in the transaction to help move the process forward.

Last Minute Surprises

I've also seen insurance company pitfalls where a property may inspect fine and the buyer accepts the current condition of the home, but then the insurance company refuses to insure the home because of the age of the roof or type of plumbing or electrical used. For example, in our area, older homes are often found to have cloth wiring (which is often not insurable) or polybutylene piping (also often not insurable), or a roof that's too aged to be covered by the insurance company. So the buyer, even if willing to proceed, can't get insurance, or has to find a costly or non-A-rated company. Even then, it's possible to get insurance for closing only to have an insurer cancel the policy after thirty days. Bottom line, knowing the many potential pitfalls early in the process is what a professional agent can help with so there are no last-minute surprises.

> *Bottom line, knowing the many potential pitfalls early in the process is what a professional agent can help with so there are no last-minute surprises.*

Speaking of last-minute surprises, one of the worst scenarios I've seen is when a buyer and seller are both ready to move out but the lender has a delay—or worse, they determine they can't fund the loan and end up cancelling the transaction. Unfortunately, there are lenders out there that don't do their due diligence upfront and find an error too late in the process, prohibiting a buyer from getting their loan. This is a huge pitfall and can have major ramifications that affect people's lives, like where everyone's going to live, how much it will all cost, and whether the situation can be worked out.

Many of these issues and pitfalls can be remedied by choosing a professional agent and using their recommended or preferred providers (lenders, inspectors, contractors, etc.), which can help the process go smoother. A professional will know how to avoid pitfalls or address them to arrive at the best solution for the client. Managing details, timelines, and contractual obligations is what a skilled agent does and what you should look for when you consider hiring one.

—— *Key Lessons:* ——————

1. Technology venture capitalists may try to find ways to streamline the transaction process, but there are many potential pitfalls that technology systems can't anticipate—having a professional agent who can guide and advise you is more important than ever.

2. A professional agent will be mindful of contractual timeframes and contingencies to protect their client from risks, like losing money or having a contract fall through.

3. Knowing what to expect during the process and receiving guidance each step of the way improves the overall client experience and leads to successful outcomes.

CHAPTER 6

CONSUMER CENTRICITY— WHERE CARE AND GIVING INTERSECT

Having a skilled professional working for you is critical to a successful real estate transaction, but even more important than that is your relationship with that agent and how consumer-centric they are. If they don't care about you, it doesn't matter how skilled they are— because likely they'll use that skill for their benefit, not yours.

We know that having an emotionally intelligent agent is critical to successfully navigating what can often be an emotional and stressful situation. We know that a professional agent offers solutions and clarity on how to move forward with your situation, negotiates like a pro when the time comes, and manages the transaction expertly.

We know that if you're selling a home, your agent should give accurate pricing advice and extensive exposure of your home to the marketplace. And if you're buying a home, a professional agent should provide guidance and explain the processes for a successful result.

These are all imperative skills an agent should have. But the key indicator to knowing whether or not you're working with a pro—and a trait you can't find through a technology portal or discount service—is an agent's willingness and ability to build a relationship with you.

In all fairness, you can have an emotionally intelligent agent who knows how to price and market a property, buy a home, negotiate well, and manage the transaction well, but who doesn't care at all about their customer. I would propose that it's hard to do the above without caring for someone, but one is clearly a set of skills, while the other is more personal. That's why having a consumer-centric agent is a distinguishing characteristic important to the list of things to look for.

Consumer centricity could be defined in many ways, and could also easily be confused with customer service. But these two terms are different. An agent can be friendly, efficient, and satisfy a client's needs, but I believe making the client happy is only one part of the equation. A consumer-centric agent goes to a deeper level beyond the transaction or customer service skills. They typically:

- put the client's needs first and do their best to help them,

- care about building the relationship first before the transaction,

- do more than is generally expected,

- know that the sale is not the end of the relationship,

- take a personal interest in the customer's life, and

- always work on improving so they can bring more benefit to their clients.

Many will agree that buying or selling a house is one of the biggest financial decisions most people ever make, which makes finding a consumer-centric agent even more important. Typically, an agent who values consumers will kick off the relationship with an initial buyer or seller consultation so they can get to know you and your needs.

Conversely, engaging an agent who rushes you to a decision and holds no initial discussions could be an indication that they're chasing their paycheck—not focusing on your interests. Although a buyer may believe that getting into a house is the priority, and sometimes that may truly be the case, what I've found is that a consumer-centric agent will help the client gain clarity of their situation by providing education and knowledge to make sure they're making an informed decision first. In a buyer's consultation, an agent should clearly explain the process, communicate the right expectations for finding a home, and plan a strategy for success that meets the client's individual needs.

In a buyer's consultation, an agent should clearly explain the process, communicate

> **the right expectations for finding a home, and plan a strategy for success that meets the client's individual needs.**

In the following case study, you'll see how I put my clients' needs first, which ultimately positively impacts the client's home buying experience.

CASE STUDY 6: EDIE WILLIAMS

When I met Edie Williams, I knew right away we had a lot in common. As a business owner and insurance agent, Edie valued customer-oriented service, and we were like-minded in our approach to working with clients. We both believed in educating and providing strategic advice instead of taking a transactional approach to sales. She and I both understood and valued the quality of relationships and helping others, and we treated our careers as a lifestyle, not a job.

At the time, Edie had a rental property she wanted to sell, and I volunteered to assess her options. She had specific numbers in mind for the sale to make sense, and as much as I would have loved to simply list the home, my primary objective was to consider her needs and see whether listing it even aligned with her goals.

Taking a consultative approach, we created a partnership whereby we watched the market and studied data in regular intervals. This experience led Edie to list her home with me when the time was right. The sale went as smoothly as possible, even though Edie had to be out of the country at a crucial time, and we had to scramble last minute to make it happen.

Edie also appreciated my company's approach to building a community support system. I know that the best way to grow a business is to build relationships that result in repeat and referral clients. Great people tend to refer great people! And I enjoy my career so much more when I'm connected to my clients deeper than just a transaction.

My goal is to create memories and positive experiences both inside and outside of the transaction—because buying and selling a home is stressful, and people don't always show up at their best and least stressed. Spending time outside of the stress of the sale is a joy for both me and my clients, and it's also a pleasure to be able to give back to those who have given so much to me and my family. When we give for the sake of giving, it's always amazing to me how our life experiences are enriched, and our business does better.

We invite our clients to family-oriented gatherings, like the ice-cream social Edie fondly remembers through the photo we took of her twins and husband.

In addition, I'm constantly looking to improve my skills and invest in my training and personal growth, because that will help me serve my clients at a deeper level. Synergizing with Edie and masterminding on how to grow our businesses following a consumer-centric model has been extremely rewarding, and it was extra special for Edie to be able to experience how I work, being a client herself.

"You offered time and energy, but then you recommended that I wait to list the property," Edie said. "That showed me that you value your customers' needs before profit. Your approach was holistic. Since you surround yourself with like-minded people, your whole team was there to support me. You have an authentic small-town approach. You give back to your clients in a quality way, and you lead with your heart, which leads to results."

You can see how having a personal relationship in this way with a client can not only improve the process for the client but also for me as an agent. An agent should be involved in this way in every step of the process.

What's Best for You

One example where I find consumer-centric agents in action is during the loan or prequalification process. For example, I have seen where a buyer may qualify for more home, but might fall in love with a house that only requires a small portion of their prequalification amount. A consumer-centric professional would encourage the client to buy the less-expensive home instead of pushing them to look for something pricier so they can benefit their own wallet.

Another instance where agents can prove to be customer-centric is when it comes to advising the seller on considering offers and counteroffers. A good agent won't push you toward the ones that lead to the fastest or highest commission specifically for their own benefit. Instead, they'll examine all of the terms of the contract and suggest what's best for you.

In addition, a customer-centric agent will provide valuable resources before, during, and after a sale. They might achieve this through emails, mail, videos, etc., so they can help enhance clients' understanding of important topics, but also to make sure the client doesn't forget them! This approach also helps deepen the connection and relationship between client and agent because it demonstrates the agent's initiative to share knowledge and educate the client. It is when no immediate financial benefit is on the line that consumers feel confident that an agent's actions are authentic and not simply transactional.

Professional Training & Growth Mindset

Another lesser-known and discussed trait of a consumer-centric professional is someone who has active interest in improving through training and knowledge.

Consumers should look for agents who attend trainings, are certified, and are constantly looking to improve their skills. These are all an indication of how seriously the agent takes their career, and how seriously you can expect them to take care of you. If you choose someone who doesn't take self-improvement seriously, you risk a poor experience because it's likely those agents aren't up to speed on best practices.

As mentioned previously, many agents practice real estate part-time alongside another full-time job. Sure, getting a real estate career off the ground is hard work and sometimes requires working two jobs temporarily. But if an agent has been part time for years, it might be an indication that they're not extremely knowledgeable about the industry, since it's not something they practice day in, day out.

To clarify, this doesn't mean all new agents don't know what they're doing; its more about how much training the agent has had and how many sales they've performed successfully versus how long they've been in the industry. An agent could practice for ten years and sell only one home versus a newer agent who's been in business one year, sold ten homes, and participates in several training conferences a year. If you decide to go with a less-experienced agent, a workaround would be to make sure they're being mentored under a more experienced agent who is actively involved in the process and is well trained themselves.

Many top-tier agents take their career seriously enough to work alongside the best in the industry. In doing so, they're able to glean best practices from peers. In fact, if you find an agent who works in a collaborative environment, for example, agents who meet as a group on a regular basis to share ideas, best practices, etc., you're likely to have found a consumer-centric agent. This type of an agent will be much better than someone who sits behind a computer and takes orders. The latter is someone who's there to complete a transaction and get paid. They are less likely to be consumer-centric.

Client Needs and Partnership

What's fascinating to me is that the National Association of Realtors reports that 89 percent of buyers would use their agent again or recommend them to others.[4] That's a fantastic percentage, except the reality is that many consumers can't remember their agent's name, making it a tad difficult to refer or use

---

4   National Association of Realtors, "Quick Real Estate Statistics," May 11, 2018, https://www.nar.realtor/research-and-statistics/quick-real-estate-statistics.

them again. It's easier just to research online and end up with an agent who has the most marketing or biggest discount, without really understanding how important the professional relationship is.

Finally, a consumer-centric agent, though they may have boundaries and scheduled time off, will remain on-call for emergencies or time-sensitive situations. Consumer-centric agents consider their business a lifestyle, not a nine-to-five job. They know when it's important to be available and they do what they can to make sure the client is cared for, even if that means working after normal business hours to handle a time-sensitive situation.

A good agent will also know how to strategize with clients and have the courage to share thoughts and realities that clients may not want to hear. When an agent values clients' needs above their own, it creates a stronger partnership where the agent can consult the client, determine their needs, and provide solution options. This is best achieved when the agent makes a concerted effort to build a relationship with the client, because that bond is what motivates them to act in the client's best interests instead of their own.

> *When an agent values clients' needs above their own, it creates a stronger partnership where the agent can consult the client, determine their needs, and provide solution options.*

Connect and Communicate

In fact, I find one of the best ways to build a relationship with the most impactful connection is to go beyond just providing resources and advice to making sure everyone has fun! Michael J. Maher, in his book *7 Levels of Communication*, explains that things like advertising and electronic communication have the least impact on relationship building, but interacting with people one-on-one in meetings or group events is one of the most effective ways to connect and communicate. A consumer-centric agent will know the power of these experiences and make a concerted effort to demonstrate they care about their clients by giving back to them, celebrating with them, having fun with them, taking a personal interest in them, and appreciating personal and family connections with them.

One example I've found to be useful is the concept of "breaking bread," which has historical roots. Urban Dictionary defines it as the following: "To break bread is to affirm trust, confidence, and comfort with an individual or group of people. Breaking bread has a notation of friendliness and informality, derived from the original meaning regarding sharing the loaf."[5]

I love hosting events for clients where we share in the joy of breaking bread. Whether it's through happy hour, dinner, lunch, coffee breaks, or even my favorite annual ice cream party or fall pumpkin patch, sharing time and treats with my clients helps us to deepen our relationships.

A key characteristic of working with a consumer-centric professional agent, I believe, is that they take a holistic "small-town" approach with clients who support them through repeat and referral business. A consumer-centric agent will not only make sure the client's needs are considered first, but they'll also sustain the relationship long-term, ensuring they remain "top of mind" for the client in a worthwhile, meaningful way.

---

5   Urban Dictionary, s.v. "Break bread (v.)," accessed December 2018, https://www.urbandictionary.com/define.php?term=break%20bread.

Ultimately, when a consumer-centric agent serves their clients, it creates a win-win for all parties both during the transaction and beyond—because the sale is never the end of the relationship with these agents. In fact, they lead with their hearts, giving back time and time again to clients and supporters and building comradery with them over a lifetime.

Key Lessons:

1. An agent can have extensive real estate skills, but the consumer's experience is enhanced when they're consumer-centric and actually care about clients.

2. Relationships with clients should go beyond just being friendly—agents should take a personal interest in the customer's life and know that the transaction is not the end of the relationship.

3. Agents who take time to personally improve through trainings, masterminds, and collaborative experiences provide clients with a greater breadth of experience than if they were to act based on just their viewpoint and personal experiences alone.

CHAPTER 7

LIFETIME RESOURCE–
AND THEY LIVED
HAPPILY EVER AFTER

To truly experience the benefits of working with a professional real estate agent, find one who has the mind-set of desiring to be a lifetime resource for clients. Many tech and discount firms focus on transactions, but great agents know there's a deeper and longer term connection to invest in.

Living close to Orlando has had an interesting impact on my psyche. I often visited Disney World as a child, young adult, and then frequently as a mother with my own child in tow. I love Disney fairytales—the formula they employ to grab our attention and make us fall in love with the characters and story is, without question, one of the best "business models" out there!

Usually, the stories consist of a conflict, an attempt to solve a problem, a breakthrough, and then a solution that delivers a satisfying conclusion. Journeying along with the main characters (and fun sidekicks) as they deal with strife and challenges they ultimately overcome to live happily ever after. Sounds like exactly what we all want, right?

And Walt Disney's formula for business success is nothing short of inspiring:

Whatever you do, do it well. Do it so well that when people see you do it they will want to come back and see you do it again, and they will want to bring others and show them how well you do what you do.

—Walt Disney

Disney's philosophy applies to my business, too: I believe it's important to do such a good job for people that they'll want to come back to me again and again, and they'll love my work so much, they'll tell their friends, co-workers, and family about me. Though I'm not in the business of theme parks or animated movies, I am in the business of making real estate dreams come true!

> *I believe it's important to do such a good job for people that they'll want to come back to me again and again, and they'll love my work so much, they'll tell their friends, co-workers, and family about me.*

In the case of the Waller family, as you'll see in the following case study, the first time we worked together proved to be the beginning of a years-long relationship where they trusted me and my judgment with their hopes and dreams time and time again.

CASE STUDY 7: THE WALLER FAMILY

By the time I met Kathy and Chuck Waller, they had already interviewed several real estate agents in search of one who could put them at ease and help them visualize what they really wanted in a new home. We talked extensively about their needs. In particular, they had to sell their home and buy another—all before the birth of their child. It was a tight window, but Chuck was pleased by the process I used to help them get clear on their timeframe—mapping milestones out on a calendar and working backward from important dates to help them know how much time they had to get their home ready, be in the market, close after receiving a contract, identify a new home, etc.—ultimately eliminating as many unknowns by providing a defined schedule.

It was critical for me to listen and ask a lot of questions so we could get clear on what they wanted. Knowing the market and setting clear expectations helped us take a complex process and simplify it with a plan. Soon, we were simultaneously selling their first home and negotiating the purchase of a new one.

My overarching goal with the Waller family— as well as with all my clients—was to build a professional, yet personal, relationship that transcended the transaction. As the Waller family tackled repairs, prepared for a new addition to the family, and pondered adding a pool, I gave them realistic advice and personal subcontractor referrals. I believe that being a client's lifetime resource for all things real estate provides long-term value and emphasizes my main goal of having a relationship that's more than any transaction.

Today, I still often serve as a consultant for the Waller family's real estate needs. I'm honored that Kathy turns to me when she has questions about the market and wonders if they should buy, sell, or wait. We crunch numbers, look at market conditions, and think about what they want to accomplish to see if it's possible.

Being in business to serve for a lifetime may not be intuitive for many in our sales-driven industry, but I think that's a short-sighted mind-set. Just because there isn't an immediate transaction in the pipeline, or even any transaction forthcoming, doesn't make the client relationship any more or less valuable. When you treat people with respect, earn their trust, and let them know you're available to help in any and all capacities, it makes the difference between just getting a job done and being a lifetime trusted resource. Helping families like the Wallers decide which improvements to consider, referring them contractors when needed, updating them on values, and helping them analyze what their next home may look like, even if it's many years down the road before they buy, has been a cornerstone to building a business for the long term for me. And one I thoroughly enjoy.

The Waller family was very appreciative of the experience. Kathy said, "You're a great listener, very conscious of what customers want, not what you want. How many real estate agents do you know who would tell you it's okay to wait, and not sell?" Kathy also noted that my company's commitment to authentic service is not only what leads them to recommend me to their friends but what's made them repeat customers. "You're more than just an agent. You've always focused on meeting our needs—selling, buying, and beyond!" It means the world to me that the Waller family consider me as their go-to resource when it comes to "house stuff," as Kathy likes to call it.

My time with the Waller family and with all of my clients is gratifying on both sides of the table, even (and, maybe, especially) when there are unexpected circumstances. The reality of buying or selling a home is no fairy tale. It's real life, real challenges, real "what the heck?!" moments. And although not every story has a perfect ending, we can all agree that living happily ever after is a worthwhile dream to work toward. For my clients, I have the passion to do what I can to keep the happiness flowing, which isn't always the case with real estate agents.

Many of them see the consumer as a "one and done" kind of deal. Most tech companies and discount firms do the same. These people and companies are transaction focused—once the transaction's over, they feel their job is done.

Real Estate Resource

I always like to think of myself as being a client's real estate resource. That means when issues or questions come up after the sale, my clients have someone to ask for advice. Kind of like my relationship with my CPA or my insurance agent. When I have questions outside of tax season or my insurance renewal period, I can turn to them and they'll help.

A good real estate agent can be a resource outside of the buying or selling process for the following:

- contractor references,

- improvements/style questions,

- overdeveloping questions,

- attorney references, and/or

- updates on values.

Being a homeowner is a joy, but homes usually require maintenance or updating over the years. Not only can these get pricey, but it's also tough to determine whether the contractor offering the quote is qualified and will do a good job. Sometimes the "best deal" may end up costing more than if you'd hired someone a little pricier to begin with. Knowing who to turn to for help can be confusing.

Because I'm active in the real estate industry, I have access to great service providers who are involved with real estate. I know my name is on the line when I refer a contractor, so I'm constantly on the lookout for excellent, high-quality providers. I have relationships with pressure washers, carpet cleaners, handymen, appliance repair people, plumbers, electricians, A/C companies, house cleaners, painters, tile installers, security system companies, roofers, moving companies, garage door servicers, landscapers, irrigation companies, tree servicers, pool companies, fireplace cleaners, deck installers, fence companies … the list goes on. I'm intentional about networking with an extensive number of contractors because I want to build these relationships and provide lifetime value and resources to my clients.

Real Estate Questions

Even when something doesn't need repairing, I often get questions like the following:

- Should I install a pool?

- Which is better, a glassed-in room or screen porch?

- I like white kitchens; is that still in style or should I go with darker cabinets?

- What type of flooring is the best if I take out the carpet?

These are all great questions, and the decisions aren't as easy as Googling the answers, because each home is unique, each client has different needs, and market demands constantly change. Ultimately, when I consult clients on how to make wise decisions on improvements and style, I base my advice on what they're looking to accomplish, their budget, the value and location of their home, and how long they plan to live in it. Making improvements on a rental property might be different than making them on someone's "forever home." The client's needs are key to helping guide the conversation.

One of the most common questions I get when trying to help clients determine their needs is, "I'm thinking of remodeling my kitchen or bathroom, how much should I spend?" If you're not careful with improvements, you could end up spending more than you recoup when you sell your home. However, there are no hard and fast rules to major capital improvements, though there are general guidelines, such as kitchens and baths routinely recouping 75 percent of the value, or adding square footage or a bathroom increases value. So, when a client considers these types of projects, I offer to review their proposals and give them the information they need to make informed decisions. The question, however, often remains: Is it possible to overdevelop or over upgrade for a particular neighborhood? The answer is certainly yes. A $30,000 kitchen remodel may be considered overdeveloping in one neighborhood, whereas in another that amount might be barely half of what it should be. A professional agent should take time to review a client's overall home situation and perhaps even review contractor quotes to see if they're in line with what the market can recoup.

Just as a client should want to work with a professional realtor, they may also want to hire a professional attorney. Particularly because, in some states, a title company can close the sale of a home, involving attorneys. Personally, I find that having a highly skilled and knowledgeable attorney on my "go to" list for questions and interpretation of contract law is a key resource. Granted, no one wants to be in a situation where they require an attorney. But, boy, oh boy, isn't it great that when you need one, you can count on a professional recommendation from your agent? However, if you use an online resource, or even a discount firm, the closing may happen "on the cheap"—possibly even with an out-of-area closing agent. How connected do you think that agent (who may not even be in the area) is to the people at the closing and how much do you think they actually care about the client's needs or doing an excellent job? My experience in these circumstances has been mediocre at best, which is why it's so important to get a great attorney reference from your agent.

Sometimes, post-closing, certain situations warrant litigation. As disappointing as that can be, I've referred clients to litigation attorneys to help them navigate difficult real estate situations that call for more aggressive legal action. The one-and-done agents are more likely to disappear when things go awry after closing. But a professional agent who believes in the lifetime value of their clients will work hard to help them resolve the issues sometimes faced.

The Numbers

One thing a professional agent should do is routinely provide annual updates on their home value for any clients who are interested in having this information. This probably comes as no surprise, but most people who own real estate like to have a feel for what their home is worth, whether they're selling or not.

Sometimes, a client who is selling their home and moving wants to know how the numbers will play into the buying side. Sometimes, those numbers make it so that moving right away doesn't make sense, which is when we make decisions to wait and watch the market. In these cases, we'll continue providing updates, typically annually, until the numbers do make sense.

The bottom line is that you should still contact your agent and get a true estimate of value, even if you aren't planning on selling right away. Even with online valuation tools at your disposal, there's no greater accurate viewpoint than an agent who knows your home best.

A good agent, although recognizing they won't get paid for providing these updates, will do so as a courtesy to show their interest in developing a long-term professional relationship with the client—and serving as their lifetime resource. My experience with this approach has been that our clients show their loyalty and integrity by using us and referring us, when they have an opportunity. So it is a beautiful win-win relationship.

> *A good agent, although recognizing they won't get paid for providing these updates, will do so as a courtesy to show their interest in developing a*

long-term professional relationship with the client—and serving as their lifetime resource.

At the end of the day, finding an agent who desires to be this resource for all things real estate is a clear sign that you're working with a professional and not a one-and-done, transaction-driven company. Not everything following a sale is perfect, and although I can't always make everything great when problems do arise, I certainly do everything in my power to help clients get on the solution side of their needs as fast and seamlessly as possible. A true professional real estate agent serves clients with guidance and trusted resources, helping everyone get a little closer to living happily ever after.

— *Key Lessons:* —————————

1. Buying or selling a home is no fairy tale, but knowing you have someone who wants to create a lifetime relationship with you will help you confirm you're not a one-and-done transaction.

2. There are many ways a real estate agent can provide resources after a sale has occurred.

3. When considering working with an agent, find out if they have an after-sale customer service program, and if so, you can rest assured you've probably got a professional working for you.

CONCLUSION

I MAY BE BIASED, BUT ...

When looking for a top-notch surgeon, people typically want the best—they'll research, do their due diligence, confirm the education level and training of the surgeon, have a consultation to determine their professionalism, and check to see if they provide a plan that's tailored to the exact needs of the patient. Often, the best surgeons are the most expensive, and the consumer would be leery of a discount surgeon or one with no practical experience or mentoring.

Yet, in the real estate industry, rarely do any of these things happen. In fact, many people mistakenly equate a discount agent or tech company provided agent with a professional one and gravitate toward the cheapest option. Or they see an agent who's heavily marketed everywhere and assume they must be good, when good marketing has nothing to do with being a skilled, consumer-driven agent.

On another note, does it seem a little self-serving that I wrote a book about the seven key characteristics to look for in a professional real estate agent, and I just happen to strive to live up to those very attributes? I hope it doesn't come across as pompous, because that's not my intention. I want to always encourage people to look for things I feel most passionate about, and that I find most valuable. What I've experienced over the years is that there are great real estate agents who have skill and knowledge and actually care about their clients. They're building a business based on a philosophy of generosity and appreciation, and want to build repeat and referral clients.

These agents are under attack by the deep pockets of technology disrupter companies that think real estate sales can be accomplished by clicking a button or filling out a form and voila!, you've bought or sold a home. Agents who are less skilled discount their services because they're not good enough to justify the value they should be bringing to the table. Consumers tend to see all agents the same way, so they'll often just choose the first person who answers their phone, responds to an email, or is the cheapest. And, unfortunately, in our industry, it's happening more and more often, particularly when the market grows hot and people think they can easily jump in and make some quick cash.

The agents that really exude the principals I've outlined in this book are rare gems and worthy of success. And no matter where you live in the United States and Canada, reach out to me and I can connect you to them.

> *The agents that really exude the principals I've outlined in this book are rare gems and worthy of success. And no matter where you live in the United States and Canada, reach out to me and I can connect you to them.*

I have a passion for elevating the professionalism in the industry and my hope is by educating the consumer on what to look for in a real estate agent, these agents will be rewarded for their efforts and work ethic, and more and more agents will embrace these principles, and the industry as a whole will be improved.

When consumers reward discount and technology companies with their business, they may not truly understand what they're missing out on. But as more and more agents embrace these attributes, it will be easier for consumers to see just what a professional real estate agent brings to the table. Over time, the agents who step up to this level will succeed and provide a guiding light not only to other agents in the marketplace, but also to consumers who will seek them out, encouraging the cycle of quality to continue. My dream is that real estate agents be considered less as sales professionals and more so as trusted advisors. At a minimum, I'd like to see the line between the two become less blurred for consumers and for them to be better educated in knowing how to choose the right agent—someone who performs at a level of excellence and competence that should be expected from our profession.

Throughout this book, you've seen how much work is required to make sure a real estate transaction goes smoothly. Having an agent who can help manage emotions—mostly the lows—will help you gain a clearer perspective throughout the process. A great agent can help you analyze all aspects of your personal scenario and provide professional solutions for the best outcomes.

Also, while an effective marketing approach may help you get top dollar for your home, an accurate pricing strategy is more important than the best marketing in the world. By now, you should know to find someone who is able to skillfully negotiate deals, keeping both the buyer's and seller's perspectives in mind to come to a reasonable agreement. Once your home is under contract, your agent should be a suave transaction manager, able to deal with the transaction elements of a sale with ease and confidence.

You should now be able to recognize an agent who will serve your needs first and be your advocate from one who acts like a hungry salesman. And lastly, you know that a great agent will think of you beyond just a one-hit transaction and make themselves available to you as a lifetime resource.

Finally, you'll, I hope, remember that all real estate agents aren't the same, and you often get what you pay for. There are some who are more knowledgeable, experienced, and eager to help than others.

So, my final words to you in helping you find the right agent for you and your family/friends/co-workers are the following:

- Read online reviews.

- Ask for references/recent sales.

- Ask your friends and family for referrals.

- Read and share this book!

Now that you're armed with knowledge, go out and seek the right agent, but keep in mind that this person should bring value and really be in it to help you win. Don't hesitate to keep hunting until you find the right one. In the end, your efforts will reward you.

WENDY GRIFFIS GROUP

It seems obvious to point out we are in the business of helping buyers and sellers with their real estate needs. But what we are *really* in the business of is building a community of like-minded consumers who value and respect our expertise and how we care for our clients, and who then become part of our lifetime tribe and refer their friends, family, and co-workers. That can only be done when the principals in this book are brought to life.

We are also members of the Cartus Relocation Network, and the Buffini Referral Network, and have access to agents who follow the principals outlined in this book and who serve their clients with skill all over the United States and Canada. If you need a referral to an agent who practices these principals anywhere in the US and Canada, definitely reach out to us!

website: www.wendygriffisgroup.com
website: www.wendygriffis.com
e-mail: griffisrealtor@comcast.net
phone: (904) 349-3133

If you want to get to know my group better through our social channels, we can be found on:

LinkedIn: www.linkedin.com/in/wgriffis
Facebook: www.facebook.com/
WendyGriffisGroup/

Our goal is to provide high-quality service to our clients: going above and beyond what is necessary in order to give our clients peace of mind, clarity, and tangible results. This excellent work ethic results in many clients becoming lifetime customers, friends, and supporters of our business through repeat and referral business. We would love to count you among them!

CPSIA information can be obtained
at www.ICGtesting.com
Printed in the USA
JSHW011313280623
43931JS00009B/254